Steven Shaviro teaches literature and film at the University of Washington. He is the author of *Passion and Excess* (1990) and *The Cinematic Body* (1993), as well as of various articles on theory, film, and contemporary culture.

Other title   in this series:

Gary Indiana
Let It Bleed

Patrols

A Theoretical Fiction
About Postmodernism

Steven Shaviro

NEW YORK / LONDON

Library of Congress Catalog Card Number: 96-68813

A complete catalogue record for this book is available
from the British Library on request

The right of Steven Shaviro to be identified as the author
of this work has been asserted by him in accordance with
the Copyright, Designs and Patents Act 1988

This edition first published in 1997 by
Serpent's Tail, 4 Blackstock Mews, London N4
and 180 Varick Street, 10th floor, New York, NY 10014

Set in Sabon by Avon Dataset, Bidford-on-Avon
Printed in Finland by Werner Söderström Oy

Contents

Preface

This book is a theoretical fiction about postmodernism. A theoretical fiction, because I treat discursive ideas and arguments in a way analogous to how a novelist treats characters and events. About postmodernism, because the term seems unavoidable in recent discussions of contemporary culture. Postmodernism is not a theoretical option or a stylistic choice; it is the very air we breathe. We are postmodern whether we like it or not, and whether we are aware of it or not. For this very reason, the word postmodernism isn't explicitly defined anywhere in my text. Its meaning is its use: or better, its multiple and contradictory uses, as these emerge gradually in the course of the book.

My approach to postmodernism is informed by the theorists I have read and written about in previous books: Bataille, Blanchot, and Deleuze and Guattari. But also by Marshall McLuhan and by Andy Warhol, whom I have come to regard as the most significant North American theorists of postmodernism, even if neither of them ever used the term. Kathy Acker and William Burroughs, exemplary postmodern thinkers by virtue of their literary fictions, are frequently present in these pages as well. And I have also been attentive to recent developments in biology, inspired by the neo-Darwinism of Richard Dawkins and by the late Morse Peckham's provocatively Darwinian approach to the study of culture. Working in the trace of all these figures, I do not propose anything like a balanced and well-grounded critique of postmodern culture. To do so would be to assert my own separation from the phenomena under discussion; but this is a claim that I find utterly unacceptable. I try, instead, to be as timely as possible; and also perhaps a bit untimely, in the sense that Deleuze has usefully rescued from Nietzsche. It's a matter of learning how to live and feel differently; or more accurately, of articulating ways in which we already are living and feeling differently, whether we like it or not. It's for this reason that I've used the pronoun "we" rather freely throughout the book, at the risk of seeming to impose a false solidarity upon the reader. All becomings are multiple, as Deleuze and Guattari insist; the "we" is one marker of this perpetual divergence. There are others; the book shifts frequently between the first, second, and third persons, and at times makes use as well of the Spivak gender-neutral third person singular pronouns "e", "em", and "eir".

Doom Patrols, then, is not a work of historical scholarship or objective description or ideology critique or in-depth interpretation. I have scrupulously followed Oscar Wilde's two fine maxims, that the critic should avoid "careless habits of accuracy," and that e should strive "to see the object as in itself it really is not." Each chapter of Doom Patrols is headed by a proper name. But these names are themselves fictional, even when they ostensibly refer to actual individuals. For they are not identities, but singularities, as I try to work out in the course of the book. Any resemblances to persons living or dead, to objects or commercial products, or to other works of fiction and the characters and situations therein, are precisely that: resemblances, which is to say simulacra, deceptive and superficial imitations, fraudulent impersonations. All accurate depictions and representational correspondences, on the other hand, are accidental and unintended, and should be taken as signs of failure on the part of the author; the aim of the book being precisely to pervert and undermine all such forms and canons of representation.

Every text, as Burroughs says, is "a composite of many writers living and dead." To a very great extent, the present book is a collage of citations. When it comes to printed material, I have carefully observed "fair use" guidelines as specified by copyright law. But of course, many other voices have also entered into the making of this book: voices found in conversations, in email correspondence, in virtual encounters, and so on. I cannot list all of my obligations, but there are many people I would particularly like to thank. Kathy Acker, for general inspiration, and for introducing me to DOOM PATROL. Tatjana Pavlovic, for overall support during the time that most of this book was being written. Roddey Reid, for careful perusal of the manuscript, and for his incisive and useful comments. Lee Graham, Leo Daugherty, and Erin Casteel, for reading the manuscript chapter by chapter, as it was written, for sharing their reactions, and for helping me to discover my own sensibility. Kirby Olson, for provocative conversation on Sade, Klossowski, the food chain, and many other things. Hans Turley, for showing me the Way to Dino. Robert Neveldine, for many suggestions regarding My Bloody Valentine, and for comments and advice on music and other matters. Barry Schwabsky, years ago, for discovering Pullman's *Galatea*; and for much comment and discussion in the time since. Carlos Seligo, for information and inspiration on the subject of insects. Arthur Chapin, for suggesting the conceit of Heidegger in Disneyland. Various friends at LambdaMOO, for listening, and for helping me to work my ideas through. Doug Brick, for guidance on Unix and the World Wide Web. Don Mitchell, Shannon McRae, and Craig Horman, for making it possible for me to set up a Web server. Victoria Landau, for the wonderful GIFs. Faye Hirsch, Laurie Weeks, Tom Wall, Susie Brubaker, Billy Flesch, Laura Quinney, Robert Thomas, Bucky Harris, Paul Keyes, Mark Lester, Therese Grisham, Brian Massumi, Sandi Buckley, and Michael Hardt, for friendship and intellectual stimulation. And Lynne Tillman, for putting me in contact with Serpent's Tail.

Needless to say, this book is autobiographical. Every word.

1. | Grant Morrison

Seattle, 1992. Don't believe the hype. I find myself stranded in this obsessively health-minded, puritanical, routinized, and relentlessly cheerful city, lifelines cut, lost without my vital supply of counteracting stimulants. Yes, some of the bands are still great, despite the insidious pressures of fame: Nirvana, Mudhoney, Seven-Year Bitch. And yes, more cartoonists are moving here every day. But otherwise, nothing. I strain to hear an echo of Burroughs' silent scream: "What scared you all into time? Into body? Into shit? I will tell you: *the word*." Say it again and again. But does anybody even remember? These prefabricated combinations of words, these carefully crafted HWP bodies, are all I can find, perhaps all there is. Don't smoke, don't do drugs, don't put up posters on utility poles, and don't sit on the sidewalk. Smile as often as possible. Above all, watch your mouth and be polite. As Kathy Acker writes of her female Don Quixote: "Being dead, [she] could no longer speak. Being born into and part of a male world, she had no speech of her own. All she could do was read male texts which weren't hers." It all comes from somewhere else. Affectless extraterrestrial zombies are in control; that's why we have a Space Needle. Living here is like perpetually scanning a set of boring personals ads. Everybody wants the same cozy evenings by the fireside, the same long walks on the beach. But it's all a facade. Organicism is a myth. Our bodies are never ourselves, our words and texts are never really our own. They aren't "us," but the forces that crush us, the norms to which we've been subjected.

As Burroughs knows, there's no getting around it: "To speak is to lie—to live is to collaborate." The only way out is the same way we came in. With postmodernism, as with drugs and pornography, the only way to get anywhere is to immerse yourself in it as much as possible, as mindlessly and as abjectly as possible, and then just sit back and enjoy it. One fix after another, one purchase after another, one orgasm after another; for there is no end to the accumulation: "the lonely hour of the 'last instance' never arrives" (Althusser). All we can do with words and images is appropriate them, distort them, turn them against themselves. All we can do is borrow them and waste them: spend what we haven't earned, and what we don't even possess. That's my definition of postmodern culture, but it's also Citibank's definition of a healthy economy, Jacques Lacan's definition of love, and J. G. Ballard's definition of life in the postindustrial ruins. It's a relief to realize that culture is after all empty, that its imposing edifices are just ruins or sound stage facades, that bodies are extremely plastic, that facial expressions are masks, that words in fact have nothing to express. For bodies and words are merely exchange-value: commodities or money. If postmodernism is indeed, as Fredric Jameson argues, "the cultural logic of late capitalism," then it is perhaps most accurately regarded as a frenzy of delirious shopping—or better still, of shoplifting. We engage in orgies of endless consumption, forever postponing the moment when the bills come due. The party never ends: S & L scams for the rich, Visa and Master Card financing for the middle class, and even occasional riots and looting for the poor. (As I write these lines, unpaid credit card debts come to more than 33% of my yearly salary; but since I don't expect ever to be able to pay these cards off, it feels as if I'm getting everything for free). It's all a whirl of extendible lines of credit, substitution of goods, and metamorphoses of capital. The postmodern economy unfolds in an eternal present. We aren't interested in duration or preservation; we devour and squander at a frantic pace, latching on to one thing only to throw it aside in favor of something else the very next moment. Everything is negotiable, everything is available for exchange. So let yourself go. Don't be a good citizen. Don't produce, expend. Be a parasite. Consume images and be consumed by them. Live off your Visa card, and scavenge in the debris.

Case in point: **DOOM PATROL**. Every month I run to the comic book store and grab the latest issue of this DC superhero comic. It's been written since 1989 (and up to the end of 1992) by Grant Morrison, with visual layouts usually by Richard Case, and ink finishes, coloring, and lettering by various others. Like most commercial comics, it is produced in accordance with a strict division of labor. DC Comics, a division of Warner Brothers, a Time Warner Entertainment Company, owns the rights to **DOOM PATROL** and everything inside it: "All characters featured in this issue, the distinctive likenesses thereof, and all related indicia are trademarks of DC Comics." I refer to the comic here only in accordance with the official legal guidelines for "fair use." After all, you can always go check it out for yourself: a new monthly issue is only $1.75. But then again, maybe not: if you haven't already seen last year's run, you probably never will. You see, these comic books aren't made to last. They are cheap commodities, printed in limited quantities on low-grade paper, designed for rapid turnover and almost instantaneous obsolescence. Comic book stores do not keep a large back stock: they order only the number of copies of a given issue that they think they'll be able to sell in the course of the month. Of course, if you have money to spare, you can always rummage through the used bins. Some people buy new comics and encase them in plastic without even reading them; they hope to sell them later for an enormous profit. The scarcity of old issues sometimes turns them into collectors' items that command high prices; a second circuit of speculation and exchange thus grafts itself onto the first one. The mechanically reproduced object has two lives: one as an ephemeral throw-away item, the other as a precious fetish. This also corresponds to two ways that comics are consumed by their audience. On the one hand, you need to leaf through them quickly, with what Walter Benjamin calls *distracted attention*: it's precisely in this suspended state that they become so strangely absorbing. On the other hand, you need to go back over them, studying every word and every panel, with a fanatical attention to detail. The letters pages of any comic book are filled with the most minutely passionate comments and observations. The letter-writers worry about inconsistencies and continuity errors, express approval or disapproval of the characters, engage in lengthy symbolic analyses, critique the artists' renderings, and make earnest suggestions for future plot directions. In this way, these books become interactive; as Marshall McLuhan was apparently the first to note, comics are "a highly participational form of expression." It's all so different from the old habits of highbrow literary culture. A comic book has fans, more than it does "readers." The medium is the message, as McLuhan always reminds us. The disjunctive mix of words and images, the lines and colors, the rapid cinematic cuts, the changes in plot direction, the tactility of newsprint at your fingertips: all these are more important than any particular content.

Grant Morrison is acutely aware of this situation. In his hands, **DOOM PATROL** runs the gamut of pop culture possibilities, consuming words, images, and styles with a vengeance. "The idea of comics," Morrison says, "is like sitting in front of your TV with a channel changer . . . Perception is a cut-up." His run of **DOOM PATROL** is a second-order, self-reflexive comic: it perverts and reinterprets the original book (written by Arnold Drake and drawn by Bruno Premiani) that appeared from the mid-60s to the early 70s (in the so-called Silver Age of comics). The old book advertised itself as "the world's most bizarre heroes"; it concerned a group of social and genetic misfits who put their strangeness to use by becoming superheroes. Morrison picks up on the theme of refusing and resisting social norms, and gives it mind-blowingly kinky new twists. The changes are enormous: the old book's naive earnestness is replaced by the tongue-in-cheek provocations of a sly hipster. For instance, the Chief of the old **DOOM PATROL** is a brilliant idealist always pontificating that "the world is full of catastrophes to be checked, evil to be fought, people to be helped," etc.; his equivalent in the new series (ostensibly the same character) is a cold-blooded cynic inclined deliberately to provoke trauma and stress among the members of his group, just so that he can scientifically observe and record their reactions. The villains become a lot more interesting as well; the Brotherhood of Evil in the original series gives way to the Brotherhood of Dada, a group that stands beyond good and evil, "celebrates the total absurdity of life," and laudably strives to undermine consensus reality in favor of "liberation, laughs, and libido." The new **DOOM PATROL** makes the old one sort of ridiculous, but without ever exuding that smug superiority (based on a self-congratulatory distance) that is so often the fatal flaw of camp recycling. Morrison doesn't disavow the juvenile fun of earlier generations of comic books; rather, he presupposes and builds upon their enjoyments. He states that one reason he was drawn to **DOOM PATROL**, in particular, was that, even in its first incarnation, "there was a certain dark and not-altogether-healthy glamour about these four characters . . . [they] slouched into town like a pack of junkyard dogs with a grudge against mankind." The old comic provides ample fodder to be cannibalized and gleefully blasted into hyperspace. And so, in the new **DOOM PATROL**, self-conscious estrangement works as an intensifier. We get more dumb heroics, slam-bang fights, and melodramatic plot twists than we ever bargained for.

All in all, it's a long way from Krypton. In the pages of Morrison's **DOOM PATROL**, we meet hermaphroditic aliens and transvestite city streets, orgone cops and psychedelic pranksters, Gnostic terrorists and insect theologians and cultists who worship Jack the Ripper as God. **DOOM PATROL** is refreshingly unconcerned with the platitudes of "truth, justice, and the American way." Instead, it rightly depicts the Pentagon as headquarters of a bizarre supernatural conspiracy aiming to institute worldwide standardization and puritanical repression. We're continually meeting sinister forces like the Men From NOWHERE, "normalcy agents" whose mission is to "eradicate eccentricities, anomalies, and peculiarities wherever we find them." Stability, normality, conformity, and everyday boredom are always the real enemies; **DOOM PATROL** deploys against them its vision of crazed flux in a decentered, goofily hyperreal world. It provides an exhilarating mixture of kitschy nonchalance and schizoid exaggeration; it is multilinear, eclectic, and self-consciously absurdist. Of course, it is garishly illustrated, with aggressive outlines and high-contrast colors, in a style that ranges from the hallucinogenic to the Gothic. The book features a shifting cast of characters, and wildly proliferating plotlines; its tone swings between parody and horror, between extravagant silliness, wickedly barbed satire, mystical revelation, and apocalyptic dread. And through it all, **DOOM PATROL** shows a marked fondness for puns and wordplay, as well as for the consumption of psychedelic drugs.

DOOM PATROL is just the fix I need. It has exactly the right mix of ingredients. Everything is in pieces, everything is borrowed or stolen. Plagiarism "is democratic," Morrison says, "because everyone can plagiarize ... The text takes on a whole other meaning when passed through a plagiarist." And so, in exemplary postmodern fashion, Morrison vandalizes, appropriates, and recycles the most diverse, incongruous sources. And not just old comics. Burroughs and Borges, for instance, are frequently in evidence. A single page of **DOOM PATROL** may also contain allusions and references to Gnostic heresies, pop music, and chaos theory, to Thomas De Quincey and Andy Warhol and Jack Kirby, to the Brothers Grimm and Salvador Dali and *Mr. Ed*, to X-Ray Spex and My Bloody Valentine and T. S. Eliot and Terence McKenna. The comic shows an amazing capacity for sucking up and regurgitating the detritus of Anglo-American (and world) culture. It annihilates categories of high and low, proper and improper, subjecting all distinctions to a continual play of absorption, mimicry, frantic accumulation, and prodigal display. It opposes the dreariness of standardized routine with its continual show of recombinant delirium.

Pastiche of this sort is a lot like dressing in drag: in both, it's a matter of piling up and juxtaposing stereotypical traits, thereby transforming them into eccentricities and quirks. Jameson somewhat misses the point, I think, when he argues that postmodern pastiche is "a neutral practice of such mimicry, without any of parody's ulterior motives, amputated of the satiric impulse, devoid of . . . any conviction that alongside the abnormal tongue you have momentarily borrowed, some healthy linguistic normality still exists." For the "blankness" of postmodern style in drag and pastiche is of course inspired precisely by our deep suspicion of "ulterior motives." The very notion of a "healthy . . . normality" is at the root of what oppresses us. We've heard this stuff about "normality" and "health" far too many times before. We're not complaining that the values people once believed in are now empty; to the contrary, we're doing our best to empty them more and more. Get used to it. Stealing is a thrill in itself; this enjoyment is the real reason for postmodern appropriation. We aim to undermine those "convictions" of authenticity and truth, of proper meaning and right order, that sometimes seem to be as dear to Marxist dialecticians as they are to bureaucrats in the Pentagon. Speaking in my own voice is a tedious chore, one that the forces of law and order are all too eager to impose. They want to make me responsible, to chain me to myself. "Man could never do without blood, torture, and sacrifices when he felt the need to create a memory for himself" (Nietzsche). But forgetting myself, speaking in others' stolen voices, speaking in tongues: all this is pleasure and liberation. Let a hundred simulacra bloom, let a thousand costumes and disguises contend.

Plagiarism, blank mimicry, parasitic borrowing, speaking in tongues: these are the tactics of exemplary postmodern works like **DOOM PATROL**. Irresponsible freeplay is our best response to a cultural landscape supposedly composed of fragments and ruins. Critics who seek to rectify this situation are nothing but ventriloquists vainly casting their voices in the Potemkin villages of normality. A pervasive, and clinically paranoid, fantasy of much recent science fiction is the obsessive suspicion that nobody (not even oneself) is truly alive: everything is an illusion, a false facade, a machine. Cliff Steele, one of the key protagonists of **DOOM PATROL**, experiences just such a fantasy when the contents of his mind are downloaded into the virtual-reality matrix of a super-computer. An emptying-out of the self answers the perception of a world in ruins. Organicism is dead, replaced by the atomization and routinization of bodily activity, and the increasing specialization and fragmentation of the objective world of science and culture. Now this fantasy is not a particularly new one, since it's already a staple of 19th- and 20th-century modernity: it's the delirium of that postmodernist before his time, Dr. Daniel Paul Schreber, as well as the "insignificant grouse against life" of the retro-modernist T. S. Eliot in *The Waste Land*. What may be new and different is the way in which we are now able to figure and respond to this situation.

Craig Owens and Celeste Olalquiaga, among others, suggest that Walter Benjamin's analysis of allegory is particularly appropriate to postmodern culture. In allegory, signs become materially insistent in their own right, detached from referential meaning; the mechanical piling up of fragments takes the place of organic completion or symbolic translation. The postmodern landscape is evoked by J. G. Ballard as a vista of garbage-strewn high-rise apartment buildings, shattered concrete littered with husks of burnt-out cars, snuff videos in incessant replay. Benjamin sees melancholia as a compulsive response to an intolerable situation: one in which everything seems to be fragments and ruins, in which we know that we are irrecuperably estranged from a supposed 'origin' to which we nonetheless continue compulsively to refer. Allegory "represents a continuous movement towards an unattainable origin, a movement marked by the awareness of a loss that it attempts to compensate with a baroque saturation and the obsessive reiteration of fragmented memories" (Olalquiaga). We imagine that these ruins once were whole, that these abandoned structures originally had a rational use, that these signs formerly had a sense, that we used to be organic bodies instead of robots. Dubious assumptions, to be sure; but as Nietzsche puts it, one has recourse to such fantasies and such arguments "when one has no other expedient." Anxious critics today, like Adorno and Eliot before them, feel cut off, with nowhere to turn; and so they shore up fragments against their ruin, seeking desperately to assuage their narcissistic wounds. But as Nietzsche knew, every proposed remedy to nihilism only increases the strength and depth of nihilism. We invent our lost objects posthumously. The more we brood over supposedly estranged origins, the more those origins take form retroactively, even as they recede from us. Melancholia is a recursive, self-replicating structure: it continually generates the very alienation of which it then complains. I want to suggest, therefore, that allegorical melancholy is less a mark of post-modernity *per se*, than it is a symptom of the desperation of traditional humanist intellectuals (whether of the Marxist or the conservative variety) who find themselves unable to adapt to what McLuhan calls "postliterate" culture. These people should get a life. In the postmodern world of **DOOM PATROL**, we couldn't care less about the decline of print literacy, of the nuclear family, of historical awareness, or of authentic class consciousness. We play gleefully in the rubble, for we know that such antiquated notions will never subvert anything; the grounds of contention and debate have long since shifted elsewhere.

Postmodernism is distinguished, then, not by any tendency to meditate on ruins and to allegorize its own disappointments; but by a propensity to invent new organs of perception and action, as Burroughs, McLuhan, David Cronenberg, Michael Taussig, and Donna Haraway all in various ways recommend. The cyborg, Haraway says, is a monstrous hybrid, "resolutely committed to partiality, irony, intimacy, and perversity." Pragmatically, this means that the fragmentation that Eliot bemoaned in *The Waste Land* has come full circle. In works like **DOOM PATROL**, dispersion and fragmentation are positive, affirmative, and even entertaining conditions. "We live today in the age of partial objects, bricks that have been shattered to bits, and leftovers. We no longer believe in the myth of the existence of fragments that, like pieces of an antique statue, are merely waiting for the last one to be turned up, so that they may all be glued back together to create a unity that is precisely the same as the original unity. We no longer believe in a primordial totality that once existed, or in a final totality that awaits us at some future date" (Deleuze and Guattari). In the postmodern world, fragments and ruins are no longer melancholy reminders of a vanished order. They've become instead the grotesque pieces of a hyperactive child's colossal erector set. And the party never ends: there's a standing invitation to mix and match the pieces as eclectically as we can. To a postmodern sensibility, there's no contradiction between cool and hot, irony and passion, playfulness and commitment, excitement and disgust, pleasure and anxiety, or camp distancing and involvement to the point of delirious obsession. I can read Kant in the morning, watch *Wheel of Fortune* over lunch, smoke a joint and cruise the mall in the afternoon, listen to Nirvana as I make dinner, use my Mac to download a program like Kant Generator Pro 1.2 (which generates endless streams of nonsensical text in the style of *The Critique of Pure Reason*) in the evening, and stimulate myself with a hot session of virtual sex on LambdaMOO just before going to bed. Postmodernity isn't just an option or a style or a particular stance. It is the very air we breathe, the viscous substance of our internal organs; "[it] is a river which sweeps me along, but I am the river; it is a tiger which destroys me, but I am the tiger; it is a fire which consumes me, but I am the fire" (Borges). It is only *within* the confines of postmodern space that contestation and resistance can ever possibly take place. For culture is not a living tradition or an orderly progression or an organic whole. It is rather a replete, high-tech supermarket, whose shelves we may ransack at will.

In the postmodern world, where everything is borrowed and transitory, identity explodes to such a point that we can't even say that it has been lost. We experience not the morbid fixity of melancholia, but the accelerated dislocation of convulsive hysteria and full-blown paranoia. We don't project allegories upon the ruins, so much as we restlessly traverse the bifurcations of Borgesian labyrinths: the infinitely divisible straight line suggested at the end of "Death and the Compass," or the proliferating multiplicities of "The Garden of Forking Paths." Here "nothing is true, everything is permitted"; every alternative gives way to the next, with no ground for choice among them. The paranoid discovery that there is no solidity or consistency in the world, that nothing is truly my own, at least frees me from the burdens of indebtedness and guilt. How much worse it would be if "virtual reality" were to become entirely actual, if all things were to achieve the fixity of final form. The same traumatic excess that produces the excruciating pain of psychotic disintegration also provides us with the vicarious, carnivalesque thrill of watching social processes twisted and magnified, as in funhouse mirrors. Does this mean that we've now reached the stage, dreaded by Benjamin, when mankind "can experience its own destruction as an aesthetic pleasure of the first order"? Say rather that the King, the totalitarian Leader, loses his head when he is reflected in these delirious mazes. Andy Warhol made multiple portraits of Chairman Mao, just as he did of Marilyn and Elvis. Is there really any difference? What Taussig calls our culture's "mimetic excess" destabilizes all fixities of signification and power. The proliferation of Pop replicas, the paranoiacally elaborate plot twists of science fiction novels, the lurid colors of comic books: these cannot be dismissed merely as distorted adolescent representations, since their 'distortions' make up the real itself. **DOOM PATROL** is less a surreal fantasy than it is a naturalistic rendering of our supersaturated cultural space. We never come to the end of simulation; there is no culminating moment (such as Jean Baudrillard melodramatically imagines) when everything has been captured, coded, and serialized. There's always the possibility, indeed the necessity, of once more upping the ante. The famous "extermination of the real," encountered in the form of a comic book apocalypse, turns out to be just a cheap plot device, a suspenseful (and ultimately ridiculous) twist designed to keep readers in a state of ungratified anticipation, the better to lead them to the next issue in the series. Don't produce, but waste and expend; for every destruction marks the birth of a yet realer real, of still another grotesque, outrageous, and irresponsible flowering of simulation.

2.

WALT DISNEY

Some people think it's important to be sincere. Me, I think sincerity is overrated. After all, even Ronald Reagan was sincere. Especially Ronald Reagan: that's why he never lost an election. It's high time we got rid of all this California New Age crap. Sincerity is a postmodern malady, an all-too-human invention. Other mammals may show genuine affection, or they may perpetrate elaborate and artful deceptions; but in neither case do they evince the warm outpourings of a frank and naive heart. Only Walt Disney, Frank Capra, or Steven Spielberg can give us *that*. Why are we suckered into it, time and time again? The whole gruesome story must be told. A strange mutation arose in our hominid ancestors, probably less than two hundred thousand years ago. Call it the Reagan gene: the ability to deceive others by first of all deluding yourself. Pull the wool over your own eyes, as they say in the Church of the SubGenius. It's really a ruse of body language. If you believe your own lies, you don't give off the telltale subliminal signs of deception, and so you can manipulate other people all the more successfully. Only an animal that lies to itself is able to be sincere.

That's why "Bob," patron saint of the Church of the SubGenius, is the world's greatest salesman. Dale Carnegie understood this trick; so did Reagan, and so does Ross Perot. Back in prehistoric times, the knack for opportunistic self-deception gave its possessors so enormous a selective advantage that it quickly spread throughout the hominid gene pool. Now, in our postmodern, posthistoric culture, it has become ubiquitous, a sort of "second nature." Sincerity is as American as apple pie, or violence, or optimism, or Amway. Have a nice day. We're all so warm and so concerned. Today is the first day of the rest of your life.

Do you remember Jim and Tammy Bakker? This is what they were all about. Sincerity is an affect raised to the second degree, a product of what Gerald Edelman calls "higher-order consciousness." It's something that's always already "in quotation marks." It's just a performance, but that doesn't make it any less heartfelt or real—quite the contrary. Drag queens greatly prize the category of "realness": they triumph when they can simulate to perfection that female gender whose organs of exquisite pleasure they so unfortunately lack. They are the truest women, for they are feminine even to excess. Method actors, too, regularly achieve heights of "authenticity" impossible in actual, everyday life. Both method actors and drag queens make themselves "as large as life and twice as natural" (Lewis Carroll), exhibiting a "cold, immutable perfection" that is otherwise realized only in butterfly mimicry (Severo Sarduy, citing Roger Caillois). And the same goes for Jim and Tammy, with their feel-good messages and their saccharine devotion to Jesus. Weren't the two of them always already in drag? No one could possibly be more earnest and more sincere. Think of the garish overload of Tammy's pancake makeup and Jim's welcoming smiles; think of the utopian nostalgia of Heritage USA, that hyperreal replication of small-town America where everything's just too good to be true. It makes me shiver with vertigo, even now. *There's* passion and excess for you. Too much is never enough. And too bad PTL ended up so poorly, with endless recriminations over (what else?) sex and money.

It's easy enough to sneer, of course. But I want to suggest that "it would be wrong" (as Richard Nixon once said in similar circumstances) to charge the Bakkers with hypocrisy. For they weren't exactly lying to us; at least, not any more than they were to themselves. It's just that they tempered their born-again Christianity with the classic American virtues of self-help and self-congratulation. Don't worry, be happy. As Harold Bloom suggests, it all goes back to Ralph Waldo Emerson. Self-manipulation through positive reinforcement is simply the new, improved, all-American version of what European metaphysicians call "the law of pure disguise" (Caillois), or the vertiginous ecstasy of simulation (Baudrillard). The all-American faith is that if you believe something hard enough, it **must** turn out to be true. "In the end," Nixon writes, "what matters is that you have always lived life to the hilt. I have been on the highest mountains and in the deepest valleys, but I have never lost sight of my destination." So follow that dream, as Jim and Tammy did with their vision of smiling suburban contentment. Even the most vapid conformity can become a thrilling adventure. And maybe Jim and Tammy overdid it; but then again, don't we all? We always push things too far and too hard, when it comes to manipulating ourselves and others. Far from losing sight of our destinations, we tend always to exceed our goals. Our very evolutionary success ironically leads us, as Sarduy puts it, into the "lethal squandering of ourselves."

When those uptight Europeans complain about American vulgarity, what they're really objecting to is this jubilantly smug and fatal excess that insinuates itself into all of our endeavors. In point of fact, they "squander" themselves as much and as lethally as we do; but they always dignify their stupidities with the factitious resonances of high tragedy. Here, things are different. We prefer to repeat history a second time, as farce. Instead of hearkening patiently to the voice of Being, strolling alongside Heidegger on a tranquil pathway in the Black Forest, we'd much rather take a raucous rollercoaster ride past the Bavarian castle in Disneyland. The smiley face is our answer to the anguish of being-towards-death. There's far greater delirium in everyday tackiness than there is in apocalyptic sublimity. As Ed Anger, columnist for the *Weekly World News*, prophetically wrote way back in the early 80s, "what scares the Kremlin bosses isn't America's nuclear arsenal; what scares them is that we'll open a K-Mart in Moscow, and the Russian people will like it." Ed Anger understood what the strategic planners didn't; for this is indeed how we 'won' the Cold War. Star Wars and the CIA had almost nothing to do with it.

But the more things change, the more they remain the same. Despite McDonald's in Moscow, and despite the opening of EuroDisney, European misunderstandings of America have only increased. Even Jean Baudrillard, that famous connoisseur of hyperreality, doesn't really get it. Baudrillard writes, for instance, that "Disneyland is there to conceal the fact that it is the 'real' country, all of 'real' America, which is Disneyland ... Disneyland is presented as imaginary in order to make us believe that the rest is real, when in fact all of Los Angeles and the America surrounding it are no longer real, but of the order of the hyperreal and of simulation." Reading such lines, I want to say to Baudrillard what Tonto said to the Lone Ranger: what do you mean "us," white man? Only an old-fashioned, *echt* European would think there's a mystery here. Actually, nothing has been concealed. The secret that Baudrillard prides himself on unraveling is already known to every American. We've never believed that "the rest is real"; just visit any shopping mall. This absolute continuity and resemblance—between Disneyland and everything else—is something we take utterly for granted. Disneyland doesn't serve the purposes of deterrence and dissuasion, as Baudrillard quaintly imagines. Like all theme parks, its function is rather one of encouragement and exhortation, or even provocation. It teaches us how to behave, in this new postmodern, robot-ridden service economy. Whistle while you work. Don't worry about health care; just put on a happy face. Like Reagan or PTL or LSD, Disneyland performs a hyperbolic heightening of ordinary experience. Think of the android Presidents, or of those talking birds in the Tikki room. It's all so bland and so pretty, and at the same time so oversaturated with sound, color, and motion, that the effect is violently psychedelic. "The Day the World Turned DayGlo," as the song by X-Ray Spex put it. Now even everyday banality can have the shattering intensity of a full-blown psychosis. Disneyland incites us to live life to the hilt; its rides take us through the highest mountains and the deepest valleys.

Everybody knows that in postmodern society money and consumer objects take on strange, independent lives of their own. In Philip K. Dick's *Ubik*, for instance, your shower, your refrigerator, and your front door all talk back to you when you're down and out; they threaten to sue you if you don't pay them what you owe for services rendered. But if you're a success, in the time-honored American way, then your own face starts to replace those of the Presidents on all the coins and bills. A similar conundrum arises at one point in **DOOM PATROL**: how much can a dollar bill buy, we're asked, and how much a painting of a dollar bill that's signed by Andy Warhol? Complain all you want; only don't say that you've been **fooled** by politicians, money, and machines. You may not like what they do, but you've known about it all along. As Scott Bukatman recounts, "in 1956 the opening ceremonies of Disneyland were telecast live; among the hosts was Ronald Reagan, who would one day be represented by a simulacrum therein." It's no accident that both Dick (*We Can Build You*) and J. G. Ballard (*Hello America*) share Disney's obsession with robot Presidential replicas. Audioanimatrons, even more than the real-life Presidents they simulate, are the apex of sincerity. They say what they mean and they mean what they say, without a hint of menacing ambiguity. Like P. B. Shelley's skylark, they neither look before and after, nor pine for what is not. They live the ecstasy of an eternal now, entirely consumed in the intensity of pure speech acts, performative utterances repeated endlessly, forever the same, and discharged without regret or remainder. Such is the Zen bliss of Zippy the Pinhead, watching his laundry tumble in the washing machine. It's the state of grace aspired to by William Gibson's cyberpunk heroes, the moment when thought and action are one. And it's the goal and promise of postmodern therapy, the *parole pleine* glimmering in the interminable distances of Lacanian psychoanalysis. But no one has achieved more in this direction than

Steven Shaviro

Disney's audioanimatrons. They've gone further than you and I, further even than the "real" Reagan. They've reached such purity in the art of sincere self-presence, that they aren't bothered by any residual consciousness at all. We used to wonder whether machines could pass the Turing test, and fool an outside observer into thinking they were human. But the real question is rather whether we humans can pass the productivity test, and prove ourselves to be as loyal and effective service industry workers as are androids. As Disney himself puts it, simulacrally addressing us from the Great Beyond of cryogenic sleep, audioanimatrons don't take coffee breaks, and they don't ever ask for raises or go on strike. Forget the old frontier, then. Disneyland—or America—is now so intensely real that it attains the condition that Burroughs ascribed only to the sinister city of Yass-Waddah: a place where everything is true, and nothing is permitted.

Yes, the magic of objects is everywhere in the Magic Kingdom. Call it "fetishism" if you must, but remember that it all takes place in plain view, without deception or repression. The prevalent theories are sadly out of date. Marx explains fetishism as a result of the alienation of the product from its producer, while Freud regards it as a symbolic replacement for an irrecoverable object lost in a primordial trauma. Both see the aliveness of objects as an illusion, as the projection of a vitality that really resides in the subject. Both say that the fetish is a substitute, a symptom of "lack," a veiled displacement of truer and more basic processes. Such theories have great explanatory and interpretive power; but it's for that very reason that they utterly miss the mark. They work quite effectively to dissolve and to 'explain away' the appearances; which means, ironically, that Disney's logic of hyperbolic appearance is the very thing that they are unable to grasp. If all you can say about a drag queen is that she's "really" a man, or that her ostentation conceals a defect, then you've missed the whole point of her performance. Burroughs offers a much better account of postmodern culture, when he says that we actually **do** live in an animate universe, where everything is alive and filled with (usually hostile) intentions. Don't flatter or comfort yourself by imagining

18

that qualities like intelligence are exclusively human traits, and that we just project them phantasmatically onto objects. That old humanist litany isn't much use anymore, now that all distinctions between nature and technology have collapsed. Qualities like intelligence and aggressivity and sincerity pop up all the time in distributed networks, as any Internet user knows. The wires swarm with daemons, and pretty soon they will also be populated by nanomachines. Commodities and "information" aren't just abstract systems of equivalence and exchange, as Marx, Freud, and Baudrillard optimistically suppose. They are now fully incarnated entities in their own rights, wholly present body and soul. Money talks, and whatever it says must always be taken literally. The "fetish" is always realer and more alive than anything it's alleged to have replaced.

Indeed, American culture is so abundantly fetishistic that it forces us utterly to redefine the concept. We saturate the world with our cheerfully animated products. The splendors of Disneyland, the excesses of Jim and Tammy, the platitudinous certitudes of Reagan—none of these can be said to supplement a lack, or to conceal and compensate for some hidden want. Haven't you heard, penis envy is out of date. American culture is entirely premised on "powers of the false," as Deleuze terms it in discussing the quintessentially American con men and forgers who populate the films of Orson Welles. Drag rules. This means, not that we are denying our origins or fleeing from the truth, but that "truth" and "origin" are no longer valid categories of judgment. The old Eurocentric modernists used to whine that "we had the experience, but missed the meaning" (T. S. Eliot). But for us, now, today, this isn't a problem; rather it's a cause for celebration. Meaning only gets in the way of enjoyment. Facts, as Ronald Reagan once said, are stupid things. America is the one country to which the European concept of kitsch never really applies. The difference between the "original" Parthenon in Athens and the Parthenon in Nashville, Tennessee is that the Parthenon in Nashville no longer supports the idea of there being any such thing as an intelligible difference between the two Parthenons. This is what Welles and

Disney both so brilliantly understood. As Deleuze and Guattari put it, simulation is not a mere process of substitution, but a vital, generative principle: the way that the Real is effectively produced. We manufacture selves—or we hire cheap Third World labor to do it for us—just as we manufacture automobiles and transistors. And in a rigorously Spinozistic sense, we must say that everything thus produced is exactly as authentic and as perfect as it is capable of being. It's real, it's actual, everything is satisfactual. So live life to the hilt; be all that you can be. Or, as Brian Massumi rewrites the slogan, be all you cannot be. Why worry about histories of loss and replacement, why look before and after and pine for what is not, when today is the first day of the rest of your life?

Mass-mediated politicians and Disneyfied audioanimatrons inhabit a strange postmodern space, a "distancing at the heart of the thing" that "is not a simple change of place," but rather a self-distancing in which the object itself is transformed into its own image or simulacrum (Blanchot). Such is the inconceivable, infinite distance of cyberspace: the distance that remains when all distance has been abolished, or the delay that manifests itself when all communication is instantaneous. This is the space-time of self-deceiving sincerity; but it's also the "ground" for a certain cool, ironic detachment, the famous postmodern "waning of affect" that J. G. Ballard (who coined the phrase) gets a perverse kick from, but that moralists and culture critics so routinely deplore. It shouldn't be called *irony*, exactly. The *Weekly World News* wasn't being ironic when it revealed, in September 1992, that Senator Sam Nunn was a space alien. It was merely taking everything literally, accepting events entirely at face value. The news about Nunn might have seemed surprising at first, but isn't it all too obvious now? It's really just a matter of technology finally catching up with our evolutionary potential. The genes for a Nunn or a Reagan had already emerged fifty to a hundred thousand years ago. But there could be no Nunn without space travel, just as there could be no Reagan without television. As McLuhan suggests, every mutation of technology opens up new virtual spaces to explore. The current electronic exteriorization of our nervous systems, together with its accompanying movement of Blanchotian inner distanciation, radically transforms the very nature of our bodies and what they can do. That's why netsex, or teledildonics, is so big today—together with tattooing, body piercing, and scarification. The surface of the body meets the surface of the screen. Virtual fucks and visible incisions alike testify to a vast remapping of corporeal space. Both sorts of ritual mark our participation in the ecstatic tribalism of McLuhan's "global village."

The supposed "lack of affect" and ironic blankness of postmodern culture "is in fact a surfeit," as Brian Massumi rightly insists. Our tendency to frame all we do and say "in quotation marks," to live our experiences vicariously and over long distances, shouldn't be disparaged as a defensive retreat or as a numbing lapse in responsiveness. To the contrary: it's in this very manner that we are best able to engage the brave new world of electronics and audioanimatronics. What you call kitsch is my way of living life to the hilt, of heightening experience to a fever pitch, of draining each moment to the lees. What you call affectless irony is for me a fabulous adventure, a rush of sexual excitement: a frenzied yet precise exploration of the unimagined depths of cyberspace, and of the expanded dimensions of my skin. So long live the new flesh. Let it howl in an orgasmic scream. When Disney rises at last from his years of cryogenic slumber, he'll discover a world in which hilarious perversions and psychedelic outrages run amok. Darius James thus envisions the scene in his brilliant novel *Negrophobia*: "A gigantic cherry-shaped NOSE, looking as if it were dipped in a crock of chocolate fondue, cleaves to the sides of Sleeping Beauty Castle. A green paste leaks from its nostrils . . . . The Disney Magic Mall is overrun with Zombies, who shamble through the ice-cream-and-candy splendor of Fantasyland and ride the Monorail over the technological wonders of Tomorrowland . . . . Disney's face blackens and melts. Underneath is a network of circuitry wire and tiny blinking lights . . . Walt's eyes flash and his head blows up. His body flares into flames . . . GOOFY'S head grins on top of a tall wooden stake. Blood drips from his eyes . . . The ABRAHAM LINCOLN ROBOT stumbles about in confusion." The master of audioanimatronics is himself a crazed robot; Uncle Walt has at last become one with his creations. This raging scatological chaos is something that only Disney's genius could have set into motion. The marketing of images, even of Disneyland's inanely racist ones, has an uncontrollable logic of its own. Our American multicultures and countercultures are themselves hyperbolic fractal expansions of Disney's delirious embrace of sincerity and cleanliness and niceness and grotesque sentimentalism and white middle American hyperconformity.

So let us say that we are ironic only through an excess of sincerity, and deviant precisely by virtue of our knee-jerk conformity, our desperate anxiety to please. The pure products of America go crazy. This ability to deceive ourselves and to be sincere—far more than language or sexuality—is the defining characteristic of what it means to be American, or to be human. Self-deception is not an effect of language or of the unconscious, but precisely the reverse: sincerity is the ongoing practice, the "technology of the subject" as Foucault might put it, that alone makes such constructions as language and sexuality possible. The psychical agencies—id, ego, superego—that populated Freud's quaint old middle-European cartography of the mind appear to us today as creaky, worn-out audioanimatrons, badly in need of replacement by newer and more high-tech models. It's simply a question of engineering—or of "imagineering," as the Disney corporation likes to put it. The point is not to resist by clinging to older visions and values—a mistake made alike by the survivalist Right and the communitarian Left. Let us rather push further and further, into ever new landscapes of simulation and delusion. Our only chance lies in this: to remake ourselves over and over again, frenetically chasing fashion, keeping up with state-of-the-art technology, and always being sure to purchase (or steal) the latest upgrades. Isn't that the American way? Even the most arcane fads can be marketed for success, but nothing stays hip for very long. The regulative principle of postmodern irony is that we can survive only by squandering ourselves, which is to say by becoming yet more cynical than our controllers. "Life is a rollercoaster," Nixon writes, "exhilarating on the way up and breathtaking on the way down." Next stop, Space Mountain. Like it or not, we're all aboard for the ride.

3.

BILINDA
BUTCHER

It's loud, very loud. Swirling, churning guitars, aggressive distortion and feedback. Endlessly repeated, not-quite-tonal riffs. Blinding strobe lights. Noise approaching the threshold of pain, even of ruptured eardrums. This music doesn't just assault your ears; it invests your entire body. It grasps you in a physical embrace, sliding over your skin, penetrating your orifices, slipping inside you and squeezing your internal organs. You're brutalized by the assault—or maybe not quite. For beyond the aggression of its sheer noise, this music is somehow welcoming, inviting, even caressing. "After about 30 seconds the adrenaline sets in; people are screaming and shaking their fists" (Mark Kemp). But then something clicks and quietly shifts, in your body and in your brain. "After about four minutes, a calm takes over. The noise continues. After five minutes, a feeling of utter peace takes over. Or violence." It could be either, it could be both: you can no longer make sense of such a gross opposition. It's like a Zen illumination, perhaps; or an endorphin high, at the moment just before death. By taking noise "way past the point of acceptedness," My Bloody Valentine guitarist Kevin Shields says, "it takes on a meaning in itself," even if "I don't know exactly what it means . . ." This isn't just a case of being overwhelmed by the sublime. You can't stand it, and you can't see beyond it; but for that very reason you get used to it after a while, and you never want it to end. As with psychedelic drugs—at least sometimes—sensory overload is only the beginning. There's a whole new world out there, beyond the experience of shock. You enter a realm of "microperceptions," as Deleuze and Guattari put it: "microintervals between matters, colors and sounds engulfing lines of flight, world lines, lines of transparency and intersection." Things rush up on you, suddenly, in waves, and then slip ever-so-slightly out of focus. Densely articulated textures fade in and out. You pick up on subtleties you didn't notice before: wavering rhythms, minor chords, muddily shifting tonalities, synthesized special effects, Bilinda Butcher's floating vocal lines buried deep within the mix. You even hear fragments of pop melodies, tentatively emerging and then quickly dissolving; it's as if they were suspended in a chemical solution. These are the qualities sometimes described as 'dreamy' and 'ethereal' by listeners who haven't played the *Loveless* CD at sufficiently high volume. But such words fail to convey how deeply embodied—how physically attentive, you might say—this music actually is. The sound may be vague, murky, "miasmatic" (Rachel Felder); but the murk is precisely rendered, a concrete, material presence. It surrounds you, envelops you, enfolds itself around you. This music is indeed 'spacey,' in the literal sense that it seems to have a lot of room inside: room to wander about and to get lost in. Everything blurs, as in a musical equivalent of soft focus; everything shades into everything else. But no, that's not quite right; rather, you're stunned by the realization that there are so many types of ambiguity, so many distinct shades of gray. Your nerves and your viscera are tingling, as they register the tiniest differences, the most minute alterations. These are changes beyond, or beneath, the threshold of ordinary perception. Your sensory organs are being stretched or contracted far outside their usual range. In such altered states, as Deleuze and Guattari say, "the imperceptible is perceived."

Of course, you don't figure all this out until afterwards. You begin to make sense of it only as it slips away. The concert is over, and now it's the relative silence of the street that hits you with the force of a shock. You feel at once exhilarated and drained. The ringing in your ears takes quite a while to subside. Everything in the world has returned more or less to its proper place, but in an eerie state of abeyance. My Bloody Valentine's music leaves you with a strange post-coital feeling: as if you knew you'd had an orgasm recently, but you couldn't remember when, or even exactly how it felt. Maybe this is what sex with space aliens would be like. In any case, the music never builds up to a phallic climax, in the timeworn manner of mainstream rock and roll and other such classical narrative forms. But it also evades—or defuses—the relentless erotic pulse of mutant dance forms like disco, techno, and rave. And it eschews as well the frustrated-boy rage and angst of the 'industrial' sound. As guitarist/songwriter Kevin Shields puts it, this music expresses, not "pure, unadulterated anger," but "kind of all emotions rolled into one." An intensity freed from specific content or focus; an erotic, bodily feel no longer tied to particular organs or zones. A sound as floating, enigmatic, and decentered—as 'ambient' and all-embracing—as anything by Brian Eno, but charged with a violent sense of physicality that Eno's music simply does not possess.

It may have something to do with changing notions of urban space. The modern urban experience, as Walter Benjamin suggested, has been one of continual shock—and of repeated adjustment to shock. This repetitive cycle is oppressive; yet it's also where Benjamin placed his hopes for revolutionary revitalization. But now, as we approach the millenium, the entire process seems to have run down, or reached a point of diminishing returns. Today, we take urban ruins for granted. Their givenness and everyday-ness—rather than any cycle of shock and habituation—is the trademark of the new, postmodern urbanism. You can trace it in the postapocalyptic sensibility of bands like My Bloody Valentine and Sonic Youth, or of novels like Samuel Delany's *Dhalgren*; but also in the glitzy architecture of the Westin Bonaventure Hotel, as described by Fredric Jameson. What these all have in common is that they have moved beyond shock, and into a new mode—a mannerism even—of dislocation. You'd feel at a loss if things weren't this confused and broken down. Disorientation is now part and parcel of your life. You are like Delany's protagonist, who can remember everything perfectly, with the sole exception of his own name. Postmodern space, as Jameson nicely puts it, "stands as something like an imperative to grow new organs, to expand our sensorium and our body to some new, yet unimaginable, perhaps ultimately impossible, dimensions." My Bloody Valentine's music rises to this challenge, expands to inhabit this new space. Call it anti-Muzak for postmodern shopping malls.

Such postmodern spaces are "anexact," as Deleuze & Guattari put it: "zones of indeterminacy" whose topology is inconsistent, whose contours are vague. But this indeterminacy is not a subjective illusion, not the result of insufficient precision. Rather, it is a perfectly objective indeterminacy: an *effect* that is well-defined in its own right, and that must be carefully produced. So too for the blurriness of My Bloody Valentine's sound. What they're after is not a rigorous musical structure, nor even a particular sonic texture, but something stranger and more evanescent: say a change in the atmosphere, an inflection of the ambiance. It takes place neither in the noise itself, nor in the performance, nor even in the bodies and minds of the audience; but somehow *in between* all these. This music isn't about virtuosity, or rock 'n' roll songcraft, or pop formalism. It seems very much an aberrant outgrowth of the punk 'do-it-yourself' aesthetic: even though nothing about it is the least bit spontaneous or improvised, and indeed the band is notorious for taking years in the studio to cut a single album. It's all in the way that everything's diffused, displaced, obliquely addressed. This music is all medium, and no message. On the *Loveless* CD, for instance, you don't get a sense of distinct, individual songs, since each track tends to bleed into the next. In live shows, the disorientation is still more radical. Glaring lights are trained upon the audience, making the band extremely hard to see. Indeed, the musicians seem scarcely to acknowledge the listeners' presence at all. Kevin's hair hangs down over his face, and Debbie Googe plays bass with her back to the auditorium. The four of them stand far apart from one another on stage, so that the band doesn't come across as a collective unity. But neither does any one of them come forward as a frontperson, to provide a point of visual and musical focus. Bilinda and Kevin eschew the cliched roles of virtuoso guitarist and lead singer; they trade instrumental and vocal lines unostentatiously and continually. In any case, there are no guitar solos to speak of, and the vocals are too indistinct for you to make out the words. Even Colm O'Ciosoig's drumming is nearly inaudible, buried deep in the mix. This band isn't driven by its rhythm section in a conventional rock 'n' roll sense. The usual hierarchy of rhythm (at the bottom, the steady foundation), harmony (in the middle, providing the armature) and melody (on the top, with leading lines and hooks) gets broken down, and reshuffled into new combinations. Often it's impossible to determine which of the musicians is producing any given sound, or even which sounds are being played live, and which have been pre-synthesized. In short, all the usual cues are missing; you are brought into forced contact with the gritty texture, the raw materiality of the music, because you can't organize your experience of it in any pre-programmed way. Your attention is continually being diverted and distracted, even as your senses are stimulated into hyperdrive. This sound is "cool," precisely in McLuhan's sense of the word: ubiquitous and all-enveloping, but at the same time so non-directive, so fuzzy or 'low definition,' that it compels you to become actively involved.

So this diffusion and decentering, this in-betweenness, isn't merely a formal strategy; it's also an experience, the way the music is received and felt. There's no longer a clear distinction between inside and outside, or between subject and object. The music has become an extension of your flesh; or better, your flesh is now an extension of the music. Your ears, your eyes, your mouth, your crotch, and your skin are absorbed into this irregularly pulsing, anexact, indefinitely extendible space, this postmodern mega-mall. The great ephemeral skin, Lyotard calls it: a labyrinth, or a hall of mirrors, continually breaking and reforming. It's really strange: the more 'alienating' the situation gets (to use that old-fashioned term), the more *intimate* it feels. Jameson calls it the "hallucinatory intensity" of "schizophrenic disjunction." Or better, think of it as an overwhelming feeling of proximity, crushing and caressing you at once. You can't quite map out this space, you can't locate yourself precisely, and you can't even distinguish one object from another. Everything is just too close to your eyes to be brought into sharp focus. The noise-laden air is suffocating; it presses down on your lungs, and scarcely gives you enough space to breathe. Yet you're trembling with excitement, or maybe with anticipation. Your flesh is all aflutter. The sound cradles and embraces you, inviting—even demanding—a sensuous, tactile response. Is it too much to say that this music feels sexy and sexual, even though it can't be identified with one particular gender? Not just because men and women share equal duties in the band. But because the sound of My Bloody Valentine has a lovely, playful evasiveness; it slips and slides easily around all sorts of distinctions conventionally associated with the binaries of gender. This music is both hard and soft, both noisy and lyrical; it penetrates and envelops you at once. You might think of it as androgynous, as simultaneously male and female. But maybe it's best described as neither. My Bloody Valentine seems to address you from some sort of inter-gendered or othergendered space: the space, perhaps, of what have become known on the Internet as Spivak pronouns: "e, em eir." Codified by Michael Spivak, these pronouns may be understood as the exact singular of "they, them, their." They compose a third person singular that retains the plural form's indifference, or indeterminacy, as to (biological, social, or grammatical) gender.

Androgyny and drag, of course, have long histories in rock 'n' roll; as does feminist gender-bending. Think of David Bowie, Sylvester, or the New York Dolls. And think of the line of transgressive female rockers extending from Patti Smith or the Slits to the current explosion of womanist rappers, riot grrls, and sexually assertive singer/songwriters. These artists have all experimented, in various ways, with subverting the conventional signs and attributes of gender. You can fuck around with masculinity and femininity by heightening them, by flattening them, by caricaturing them, by placing them ostentatiously in quotation marks, or by crossing or conflating them in ways that violently flout our usual expectations. In short, by turning them self-consciously into a spectacle or a performance. But something else is happening with My Bloody Valentine. Their sound works not so much to ironize performatively upon those old gender binaries, as to fritter them away into inconsequence. You can no longer tell which traits are male, and which are female. Aggressive noise and ethereal lyricism, for example, are not hard and fast opposites, but delicately different degrees along a single continuum. You slip so quickly and easily from one into the other, without even noticing the transition. And so with all the attributes that we ascribe on the basis of gender. It's not that all bodies feel just the same in the dark. But rather that, when you caress another body in the dark, the differences are so precise and immediate, so subtle and numerous, as to defy classification. What is the exact angle of this thrust, what are the specific contours of this caress? Where, on my skin, in my nerves, in my brain, do I feel this particular tingling? Who is to determine whether these curves on my chest are large enough to be called breasts? Or whether this swollen appendage is a clit or a cock? I can't even say that this body is 'mine' any longer. For here, now, is an eroticism that unsettles all markers. You could imagine this touch, if you insisted, extending onto the body either of a man or of a woman, or even of some other, alien being. But why insist? This pressure, this texture, this smell, this gesture, is altogether fortuitous and unique. There's nothing that you can recognize and identify any longer. What comes before the name?, asks the eponymous character in Godard's *First Name: Carmen*; who am I before I have a name? A question to which there isn't any answer. These feelings, these caresses, these convulsions, are so singular as to be altogether anonymous.

There are times—when you're tripping, or when you're in the back room of some bathhouse—that names and nouns just don't seem to matter any longer. That's the indistinction of Spivak pronouns, and of My Bloody Valentine's sound: an active, singular indeterminacy. Spivak pronouns are neither male nor female, but they are marked, in contradistinction to the genderless general term that is the neuter. The neuter is something fixed; but the Spivak is always in between or in transition. Kate Bornstein thus defines eir transsexual experience as the condition of being "a former-man and not-quite-woman." Deleuze and Guattari call it the time of Aeon: "the indefinite time of the event, the floating line that knows only speeds and affects . . . A simultaneous too-late and too-early, a something that is both going to happen and has just happened." Such is the shifting, fractured pulse of My Bloody Valentine's music, always displacing or pulling away from itself. It's not a question, then, of uniting masculine and feminine traits in some supposed higher unity; nor is it one merely of moving from one pre-existing gender position to the other. It's rather a matter of teasing all the various traits apart, in order to mark out and inhabit an entirely different terrain. As Allucquere Rosanne Stone puts it, the goal and "essence" of transsexuality used to be defined as success-fully "passing" as a member of one's second, adopted gender. But the new "post-transsexuality" will have none of that. It's a joyous and singular passage, rather than an anxious ritual of passing: an active, never-ending metamorphosis. Spivak sexuality has no fixed, prior definition; it's something that needs continually to be (re-)invented. The point, Stone says, is "to map the refigured body onto conventional gender discourse and thereby disrupt it, to take advantage of the dissonances created by such a juxtaposition to fragment and reconstitute the elements of gender in new and unexpected geometries." Corresponding to the time of Aeon is a fractal space of gender fluidity, one that the old binaries (or Cartesian coordinates) are no longer able to define.

Of course this is a physical process, and not just a conceptual one. It isn't the least bit contradictory for Bornstein to insist both that gender is an arbitrary social construction, and yet that eir own transformation needed to be accomplished materially, with the help of medical procedures. It's the flesh, after all, that suffers under the weight of these constructions; and it is in the intimate folds of the flesh that we may best discover the wherewithal to resist. Hormone treatments, mammoplasty, and penile inversion are all parts of the grand experiment. We must learn to refit our organs for new uses; as Deleuze and Guattari say, it's all a matter of bodies and their flows. Often quite literally so. Bornstein recalls one moment during the surgery, when "the urethral opening is pushed over to the side, so you don't know in which direction you're going to pee . . . So when I sat down to pee, it shot straight up in the air, and I was like, 'Oh nooooooooo!'" Isn't it in much this same way that the musicians of My Bloody Valentine recast the potential of their musical instruments? Unexpected noises shoot off in all directions. It's like a penile inversion performed upon the guitar. That great boy-fetish-object of rock is detourned from its usual macho gestures and rhythms. Synthesizers, too, are demasculinized, made to float loose from their typical Gothic or industrial trappings. It's what you actually hear that counts, not how it was made, or who owns it, or what it all means. Kevin and Bilinda revel in the sheer density and variety of sounds that their instruments are able to produce. Why restrict ourselves, after all, to so few, and to such narrowly gendered, erogenous zones? Sound effects are to be fooled around with, just like sex toys. Don't be intimidated, don't follow rules, just mix and match your own. Smash yourself headfirst into the wall of sound. Enhanced materiality means expanded pleasure. Technophilia, yes, but in a new sort of way. For playing like this is far removed from the boys-will-have-their-toys attitude that one so frequently encounters. For once, hi-tech isn't a weapon or an arcane secret or a sign of coolness or a nerdy obsession. It isn't even much of a novelty any longer; it's simply part of the landscape, a set of available tools. Machines have lost their hard, phallic edge. For Kate Bornstein and My Bloody Valentine alike, it's as if this technologized, ambiguous, singular Spivak body were finally as vital, as immediate, and as natural as any other—which of course it is.

What desire is at work here, then? What passion drives this music? Whence this appetite to anonymize and reconfigure oneself? Here's where I think of Rebis, the odd one out, the most enigmatic member of the **DOOM PATROL**. Rebis's body is provocatively ambiguous, with feminine breasts and torso, but masculine hips. E is swathed from head to foot in tightly-wrapped protective bandages, from beneath which escapes a greenish radioactive glow. Above that, e's dressed in fashionable high-heeled boots and a long trench coat, with pointy designer sunglasses floating a few inches before eir eyes. The effect is alluringly svelte, but also distant and cold. There's no way to get through to em. Rebis seems untouched by merely human concerns; e affects an air of icy, almost reptilian detachment. E emanates an auratic force field that renders em invulnerable, and apparently also insusceptible to sympathy or pain. Even when the **DOOM PATROL** is in the midst of a crisis, e can scarcely be prevailed upon to act. There's no arguing with em, or entering into dialogue; eir speech seems to come from an unreachable distance (as is marked on the page by drawing eir speech balloons with jagged edges). Everything about em, then, is just too cool for words. And this charisma is a direct result of eir intergendered history. Rebis is formed from the unwilling union of two initially separate human characters: one a white male, the test pilot Larry Trainor, the other a black female, the doctor Eleanor Poole. They are joined into one flesh by the work of a third entity: the mysterious "negative energy being" called Mercurius. This abstract, impersonal presence, like a vampire or a virus, appropriates their bodies in order to replicate itself. In medieval alchemy, the hermaphroditic body was a crucial link in the quest for the philosophers' stone. Larry and Eleanor thus find themselves in an "alchemical marriage": a stifling, fatiguing, and tortuous erotic union. It's bad, unsatisfying sex that nonetheless goes on forever, well beyond the point of exhaustion. Unceasing turmoil, without hope of repose. Constellations are shattered, but "the war in heaven never ends." Personal identity is violently reconfigured: "bodies and spirits pounded in a mortar, thoughts and memories crushed together, blended and refashioned." And this traumatic agitation is the key to Rebis's seductive coolness. Eir distance from others only echoes the distances e includes within emself. Turmoil and detachment are two sides of the same coin: they both express a passion that is no longer grounded in the merely personal. It inhabits the vast spaces between persons instead, making a life for itself in those indeterminate zones. In one sense, the postmodern "waning of affect" has never been carried further. But Rebis, like My Bloody Valentine, intimates a new way of life, where this waning is no longer felt as a deprivation. Rebis works through eir all-too-human anguish on the sterile surface of the moon; but e returns triumphant, renewing emself so that the whole process can begin again. We last see Rebis as e disappears into eir own alternative realm, "a world of infinite novelty," where "it's impossible to visit the same place twice." A world that continually reforms itself in kaleidoscopic patterns.

"During the 60s," Andy Warhol writes, "people forgot what emotions were supposed to be. And I don't think they've ever remembered. I think that once you see emotions from a certain angle you can never think of them as real again." Has there ever been a better definition of the advent of the postmodern? Once you've reached that certain angle, there is no going back. That's what happens to Rebis; it's also, I think, what's at stake in My Bloody Valentine's music. Don't think it's all just a matter of jaded cynicism, disillusionment, and loss. There's a freedom that comes from escaping, or unlearning, what we've always been told our emotions are "supposed to be." And there's real intensity at work in the process of actively forgetting. The pain and turmoil of My Bloody Valentine's sound unfolds at a vast distance: it's oddly self-contained, beyond shock and beyond angst. But this very distance—this coolness, this suspension, this sense of floating in a void—is in its own right a visceral experience. If our emotions are no longer "real," it's because they are no longer strictly personal; we've passed a certain threshold, and entered this new, singular, anonymous space. It's a space, yes, of uncertainty and longing, of detachment and dissociation. But in such a postmodern landscape, passion and irony are indissociable; to quote Bataille quoting Nietzsche, "the night is also a sun." The concert is over now; I'm tired, I'm drunk, and I'm stoned. I have, I must admit, only the vaguest idea of what happened. I'll probably recall even less when

I wake up with a hangover tomorrow. But somehow this seems appropriate for a music that doesn't prefer one mood, one gender, one position to another. A music poised equally, as Kevin Shields says, between "self-assertion" and "self-obliteration."

4.

MICHEL

FOUCAULT

Somebody wrote a letter to Ann Landers once, asking about oral sex. "Does it mean they just talk about it?," the pseudonymous "Housewife from Maine" wanted to know, or was something more involved? Ann Landers replied that oral sex was a perfectly healthy and normal human activity, not a perversion, and that there was indeed more to it than just talk. She urged "Housewife from Maine" to "use your imagination" to figure it all out, given that the details could not be printed in a "family newspaper." As a last resort, Ann recommended consulting her entry on the topic— complete with up-to-date, expert medical advice—in *The Ann Landers Encyclopedia*.

This story, I think, would have delighted Foucault, for it envelops all his theses on sex and power. "Housewife from Maine" was righter than she knew: sexuality is indeed "oral" in our culture, in the precise sense that it is continually being channelled into discourse. Sexual practices are judged and characterized in relation to certain behavioral norms, submitted to the authority of medical experts, and read as signs or symptoms of basic personality structures. They are given their proper places in Ann Landers' Encyclopedia, with its strange mixture of inspirational anecdotes, medical advice, and lessons in etiquette. "Oral sex" is not named in any cruder or more direct language, out of a grotesque deference to the sensibilities of the nuclear family; yet the way in which it is 'repressed' actually works to titillate the reader. Sex is not a bodily activity in our society, a matter of pleasures and pains, so much as it is the locus of a certain "truth," grist for the mill of a massive apparatus of knowledge. We have had the meaning, but missed the experience. What would happen, after all, if "Housewife from Maine" took Ann's advice and used her imagination? Foucault's whole endeavor is to make us aware how limited our imaginations really are, especially when it comes to sexuality. As Deleuze says, paraphrasing Spinoza, we still do not know what our bodies can do. Even our wildest s&m fantasies are all too often trite and formulaic. This is why Foucault ultimately concludes that "sex is boring." His *History of Sexuality* is an account, not of sexual practices themselves, but "of the manner in which pleasure, desires, and sexual behaviors have been problematized, reflected upon and thought about" at different times and across different cultures. It's an amazing story of contingencies and mutations, of violence and cunning, of continual innovations in methods of control, of exquisite refinements in the arts of cruelty. No structure of power relations remains stable for very long; no position can be taken for granted, and no outcome is preordained. It's a long way from Athens to Berkeley; the "care of the self" in ancient Greece is almost "diametrically opposed" to "the Californian cult of the self." Obsessive self-examination, focusing on sexual behavior, is of course central to both; but in the service of altogether different motives and values. The one preaches moderation and self-fashioning, the other authenticity and self-discovery. It's hard to decide which is worse. Yet for all these historical differences in paradigms of self and sexuality, the real problem is that things never change enough. Problematizations differ, but concrete behaviors do not. What finally most depresses Foucault is the monotonous sameness of sexual practices and behaviors, from one time and culture to another. Always the same positions, the same rhythms, the same rituals, the same binary divisions of gender. Foucault discovers, beneath our apparent sexual variety, an appalling paucity of imagination and invention. Hence his famous call, at the end of *The Order of Things*, for the disappearance and "absolute dispersion of Man." And hence the epigraph from René Char, which graces the second and third volumes of *The History of Sexuality*: "human history is a long sequence of synonyms for the same word. It is our duty to contradict this."

Far from simply exalting cultural difference, we might do better to ask why human cultures aren't *more* diverse than in fact they are. From a biological standpoint, our sex lives are exceedingly dreary. Other organisms are far more inventive. Consider, for instance, the bedbug (*Cimex lectularius*). The males of this species fuck by stabbing and puncturing their conspecifics' abdomens. Every copulation is a wound. The victims of these aggressions, males and females alike, are permanently scarred; and they carry their rapists' sperm in their circulatory systems for the rest of their lives. As Howard Ensign Evans puts it: "the image of a covey of bedbugs disporting themselves in this manner while waiting for a blood meal—copulating with either sex and at the same time nourishing one another with their semen—makes Sodom seem as pure as the Vatican." Even Sade never imagined such a scenario. No Californian cult of the self here! We humans should be thankful that bedbugs regard us not as sex partners, but only as food. —But if all this penetration seems too obnoxiously macho, then consider instead the whiptail lizard (*Cnemidophorus uniparens*) of the American Southwest. This species is parthenogenetic: it consists entirely of females, who reproduce without any need for sperm. But that doesn't stop them from engaging in "pseudocopulation": they mount and thrust at one another, variously adopting what in other species would be considered 'masculine' and 'feminine' roles. Though no genetic material is actually exchanged, this gender role-playing has real physiological and reproductive effects: animals who have pseudocopulated are far more fertile than those who have not. "Simulated" sexual acts produce measurable hormonal changes. Drag performance is essential to these lizards' life cycle.

Such delightful or gruesome anecdotes fill the pages of natural history. Where did we ever get the strange idea that nature—as opposed to culture—is ahistorical and timeless? We are far too impressed by our own cleverness and self-consciousness. But "human sex," Lynn Margulis and Dorion Sagan remind us, "is just one example among thirty million or more kinds of sex." We need to stop telling ourselves the same old anthropocentric bedtime stories. "Man is a recent invention," as Foucault insists; the history of sexuality long predates our all-too-human concerns. Margulis and Sagan trace its prehuman genealogy. Sexuality first appeared in the world as a form of primordial cannibalism. In the anaerobic earth of three and a half billion years ago, terrorist bacteria preyed relentlessly on one another. Every random encounter was fraught with violence and danger. Cells continually penetrated and devoured other cells. "Everywhere poisonous mixtures seethed in the depths of bodies; abominable necromancies, incests, and feedings were elaborated" (Deleuze). But at some point, a certain aggressor cell had an attack of indigestion. Its victim's DNA resisted digestive breakdown. Instead, it continued to manufacture proteins in its new environment of alien cytoplasm. No cellular reproduction had occurred, yet a new, monstrous hybrid was born: the first sexual being, the first infection. The universal feeding frenzy was transformed into a delirious erotic intermingling: "cannibalism became fertilization, and meiosis was forced to evolve" (Margulis and Sagan). And that's why plants and animals have gonads today. It's also why our cells are stuffed with organelles: mitochondria that let us breathe oxygen, chloroplasts that plants use to photosynthesize. These are all contingent effects of unplanned, miscegenetic encounters: the evolutionary fallout of prokaryotic sex.

Microscopic sexuality is indeed no fantasy. Margulis and Sagan gleefully detail the "fluid promiscuity" of bacteria, the conjoining and communication of their bodies, a perpetual orgy that puts all eukaryotic sexuality to shame. "Bacterial cells donate and receive genes in the form of viruses and plasmids all the time": there's no clear distinction between copulation and infection. Bacteria also have no fixed gender; they engage in a continual "travesty of transvestism," repeatedly trading "fertility factors" back and forth. Bacterial DNA is easily exchanged, transmuted, and recombined, because it floats freely through the cell, rather than being locked up inside a nucleus. Bacteria are as it were 'naturally' decentered; only they experience this decenteredness as something other than the loss or lack of a center. The earth's most primordial inhabitants, they are nonetheless free from any concern about origins, any metaphysical nostalgia or Heideggerian yearning. Our human ontological insecurity is largely a result of our projecting upon the cosmos certain heterosexual male anxieties over procreation and paternity. How stereotypically mammalian! In bacteria, to the contrary, sexuality and reproduction are entirely distinct. They reproduce asexually, by simple fission; they have sex non-reproductively, in a furor of genetic exchange. It took a long and painful evolutionary history, stretching over billions of years, finally to link sex and reproduction together. What a strange conceit, to imagine that this linkage is somehow pre-given or 'natural,' inscribed in the very order of things!

So no, I won't play culture to your nature; it's time to have done with the whole idea of their distinction. Deleuze and Guattari show us the schizo on his walk, at a point "before the man-nature dichotomy, before all the coordinates based on this fundamental dichotomy have been laid down . . . There is no such thing as either man or nature now, only a process that produces the one within the other and couples the machines together . . . To be a chlorophyll- or a photosynthesis-machine, or at least slip your body into such machines as one part among the others." Margulis and Sagan similarly imagine a "benevolent venereal disease," symbiotic algae that would "invade the testes" of male humans "and from there enter sperm cells as they are made." The result of such males' mating would be a new species, *Homo photosyntheticus*, "green" humans with the plant-like ability to manufacture their own food out of air and sunlight. As evolution proceeded, such humans would "tend to lose their mouths," which would no longer be needed for feeding. Instead, they would become ever more "translucent, slothish, and sedentary": sort of 'ecologically correct' junkies. Indeed, algae specialist Ryan Drum proposes just such a symbiotic merger as a better alternative to America's war on drugs. Future green addicts, strung out on sunlight, could both nourish themselves and produce their own pharmaceuticals; thus "they would no longer be a burden to society." It sounds like a scenario straight out of Burroughs; but Margulis and Sagan insist that it's technologically feasible.

"Deployments of power," Foucault says, "are directly connected to the body—to bodies, functions, physiological processes, sensations, and pleasures." It's a reductive mistake to separate culture from the body, to "take account of bodies only through the manner in which they have been perceived and given meaning and value." Psychoanalytic theorists have gotten it exactly backwards. They imagine a body that simply lies there, outside of history, mute and changeless, until it is "inscribed" by the mark of the Symbolic order. Until, that is, it's been inseminated by the Phallus. They claim it's our entry into language and culture that unbinds sexuality from reproduction, that unlinks desire from simple need. Embarrassed by their Founder's notorious dictum that "anatomy is destiny," they choose instead to ignore the body altogether, claiming that the Phallus has nothing to do with the penis. But has anyone ever really been able to maintain such a separation? If anything, culture makes for a far harsher "destiny" than does anatomy. Socially enforced norms of human behavior tend to be more rigid and intolerant of change than 'natural' constraints ever were. Nowhere in the biological world are sexual acts bound so closely to reproduction as they are in human "symbolic exchange." The Symbolic order of culture and language is precisely what reduces desire to need, sex to exchange-value, bodily pleasure to the demand for truth, expenditure to production. "I fear we are not getting rid of God," as Nietzsche said, "because we still believe in grammar." It's our discourse, for instance, that divides us into merely two sexes; from an anatomical viewpoint, such a dichotomy is ridiculous. Anne Fausto-Sterling counts at least five anatomical genders: herms, merms, and ferms, as well as females and males. But she adds that this is still a reductive classification; our bodies embrace "a vast, infinitely malleable continuum that defies the constraints of even five categories." Nonstandard or intermediate genders are far more common than you might think: indeed, Fausto-Sterling says, they "may constitute as many as 4 percent of all births." But most often the othergendered are immediately "entered into a program of hormonal and surgical management so that they can slip quietly into society as 'normal' heterosexual males or females." Such is the actual effect of the supposed autonomy of language and culture. If your flesh doesn't obey Lacan's Law of binary difference, then your compliance will be enforced with drugs and the surgeon's scalpel.

But disciplining the flesh in this kind of way is a repetitious and never-ending task. In the pages of **DOOM PATROL** we meet the Sex Men, hardboiled, macho cops with orgone-blue skin whose 'thankless' toil involves reining in all forms of bodily excess, and reabsorbing the unproductive residues of sexual energy. Grant Morrison wittily reduces the old melodrama of sexual liberation versus societal repression to the banal form of a police procedural. These guys just wearily shrug their shoulders at the most outrageous spectacles of eroticism unhinged; they've already seen it all. No need to worry; it's "just another day for the Sex Men." Such workmanlike tedium only points up Foucault's observation that power is never in place once and for all. Its "gray, anonymous" procedures have to be instituted afresh every morning. Power builds repetitiously, from the bottom up; its very inertia implies the inevitability of resistance. Overt discourses of liberation are less of a threat to power than is the simple dumb tenacity of the flesh.

There's no way around it, after all. Bodies stubbornly resist psychological or linguistic categorization. Organs sprout and grow, adapt themselves to new functions, even uproot themselves and migrate to new locations. Orifices open and close. Our bodies still retain the marks of the old bacterial freedoms, even when our institutions work busily to suppress them. On the surfaces of the skin, and in the depths of the viscera, we may discover the excesses of an inhuman sexuality. Foucault thus proposes the sexuo-linguistic theory of Jean-Pierre Brisset as an antidote to the anthropocentric structuralisms of Saussure, Lacan, and Chomsky. Brisset maintains that human beings are immediately descended from frogs. He supports his claim with exhaustive linguistic analyses. Our speech, he shows, is a hypostasis of frogs' croaking in the mudflats; our writing conserves the traces of their obscure hatreds, jealousies, and battles. Brisset, much like McLuhan, affirms the *tactility* of language, its oral and aural density, its rich, viscous materiality. He "puts words back in the mouth and around the sexual organs." Language arises out of orgasmic screams and bodily spasms. There's no clear dividing line between body and thought, or nature and culture, just as there is none between the water and the land. Language and sexuality are not the clean, abstract structures the so-called "human sciences" have long imagined them to be. Rather, they are forces in continual agitation in the depths of our bodies.

Our bodies join and separate: this is the mark of the social, whether in frogs or human beings or prokaryotes. To speak of human culture is much the same thing as to speak of a "culture" of bacteria. Only those dazzled by Gutenberg's movable type, or by the concurrent figure of "Man," could ever have imagined otherwise. But now "Man" is on the verge of disappearing: he is gradually being erased, as Foucault puts it, "like a face drawn in sand at the edge of the sea." Today, we no longer believe in the uniqueness of human language; we are no longer willing to obey the modernist injunction "to know sex, to reveal its law and its power, to discover it, to liberate it, to articulate it in discourse, to formulate it in truth." The new electronic and informational technologies have permeated and 'denatured' our world; this transformation invites us to imagine "a different economy of bodies and pleasures," one no longer subjected to what Foucault mockingly calls "the austere monarchy of sex." In postmodern culture, as Deleuze says explicating Foucault, "the forces in man enter into relation with forces from the outside, those of silicon replacing carbon, of genetic components replacing the organism, of agrammaticalities replacing the signifier." Such outside forces are now the only "nature" we know; they define our very being. Human culture is in large part a machine—a technology, a software—for experimentally simulating the effects of biological evolution. Alas, in most cases we don't do all that good a job of it. Even our cutting-edge engineering projects—like gene splicing and nanotechnology—thus far have only feebly echoed everyday bacterial practices. But we make up somewhat in rapidity of change for what we lose in power and efficiency. We've done in a mere few hundred thousand years what took microorganisms billions. And we have at least equaled bacteria when it comes to such things as waging war, or extending ourselves across the face of the planet. We are continually elaborating newer, more intricate forms of communication. Our touch is, by turns, invigorating and mortal. We exchange memes in the night, with our bodies' erotic contact, just as bacteria exchange genes.

"All media work us over completely," McLuhan warns, "leaving no part of us untouched, unaffected, unaltered." At the utmost extremities of human thought, Sade, Bataille, and Klossowski envision a thick and endless carnality, a universal prostitution and interpenetration of bodies. They imagine an exchange not bound by any equivalent. They imagine a loss so great that no recompense can match it. They imagine a perpetual crossing of limits, transgression without resolution. They imagine a communication forever consuming its contents, until it is all medium and no message. They call it bliss; they also call it infection. We don't look back; we wallow in our own shit and piss. But aren't these precisely the conditions of bacterial sex? It isn't a question of going back, which in any case would be impossible. But of reaffirming the traces, within our own bodies, of all these "oral" forces: engorgement, cannibalism, aggressive absorption, monstrous incorporation. Even today, sex circulates through our mouths, is savored on our tongues, and works its way deep into our rectums. If modern biopower operates by channelling sex into discourse, then one way our bodies resist is by resolving language back into raw flesh. Such is the implication of Laurie Weeks' short story, *Swallow*: "I often said things I neither intended nor felt, as if words congregated in my mouth, foreign particles, to swarm forth and engulf me in a sticky murk . . . I had begun to get words mixed up with food; if it came inside my mouth, a thing seemed to have the ability to change me in unpredictable ways . . ."

Hands are for grasping, or tearing, or caressing; but mouths, lips, and tongues bespeak a still greater intimacy. You don't hold an object in your mouth—a cock, a clit, a gobbet of meat, whatever—the same way that you would hold it in your fingers. Something *else* happens when you lick, bite, suck, or swallow, something that changes you in unpredictable ways. I'm flooded with cum and saliva, until I almost gag; I savor the taste on my palate as long as I possibly can. Or I feel the raspy tongue of the cat sliding across my skin. Watts Martin's furry porno story, "Satisfaction," tells of a male human being who fucks a female tiger morph. For all his macho pride in his own sexual prowess, nothing he does is able to satisfy her lust. Finally she pins him down and devours him piece by piece: "Her eyes were no longer even those of a dominatrix looking at her partner; they belonged to a carnivore playing with her trapped prey . . . She brought his hand to her mouth and ran her tongue across it, then bit through at the knuckles, spitting the fingers onto the floor . . . She tilted her head down and started nibbling off flesh, this time in small bites instead of one large one . . . The pain crossed some point where it seemed he no longer felt it, or perhaps forgot what it was like not to be feeling it at all . . . She seemed to be climaxing almost continuously, moaning and purring as she ripped through his legs, swallowing them in ragged chunks and lapping up the blood."

Predation on one side; ecstatic dismemberment on the other. Sex is not the deep secret, the hidden truth of our being. It isn't communion; it doesn't bring us together. It detaches us from others, and even from ourselves. Uproot it, then, from its place in *The Ann Landers Encyclopedia*. Foucault urges us to reject the ingrained Cartesian notion that there is "something other" in sex, "something else and something more," than bodies, organs, and their sensations and pleasures. Fucking is the last thing that will ever tell you who you are. It's not a return to roots, but an ongoing performance: an endless improvisation of things "neither intended nor felt." Foucault calls it a way to "get free of oneself" (*se déprendre de soi-même*). In the postmodern world, sex is no longer a fatality. It's an intense circulation of alien pains and pleasures, of unknown powers and vulnerabilities, of surprising engulfments and disgorgements. "Sex organs can sprout anywhere," Bucky Harris writes, "and one stroke of the tongue can be as electrifying as a fist up the ass." Furries and scalies come in all shapes and sizes; things can get pretty frantic at FurryMUCK. But furry sex is just one way to go; there are others. If you aren't into all that hair, you might find shaving the pubes a turn-on. Or you can become a vampire, if you prefer blood to cum. If you don't like leather, then try rubber: a different substance, a different feel, a different set of sensations. All these are not fantasies, but actual *work on the body*. When you open your mouth—or your ass, or your cunt—there's no way of knowing what "foreign particles" will enter. And when you entrust your body to someone else's mouth, ass, or cunt, all you know is that, whatever else happens, you won't emerge unscathed. Sex isn't fusion but confusion, as Sonic Youth once put it. You are never more alone, more *separate*, than when you shudder in orgasm. But afterwards, back in touch with the world, you find that your body has somehow been strangely altered: "My gums bled into his palms, which he cupped," recounts a narrator in Laurie Weeks' *Swallow*. "I wanted to pour the blood back into his body, which was mine . . . I wanted to spit my teeth into his palm, a gift . . . I took an odd satisfaction in this state of affairs. I felt that now my disease spoke for me, that it reflected the seriousness, the depth, that my flesh and childish prattle used to hide. I listened to records, read poetry . . . I smoked Marlboros and vaguely felt my lungs soften, bits of them begin to drift toward my feet."

5. HERSCHELL GORDON LEWIS

Let's say you don't feel happy with your life. Let's say you don't feel comfortable in this body. Let's say you don't feel in control of your actions. Your nerve endings tingle with continuous, unwanted arousal. The merest glance, a figure passing in the street, and all of a sudden you become hard or wet. Every object in your visual field glimmers with a halo, an aura: the harbinger of an impending epileptic fit. Cells divide, faster and faster, a cancerous tumor eats away at your brain. You find yourself the prey of physical convulsions, epidemic infections, and monstrous growths; or of nervous tics, misdirected actions, and inappropriate reactions. Your body has a life and a will of its own: you can't stop yourself from killing again and again, from gulping down more and more sweets, from spewing forth a torrent of obscenities. Your body is a puppet, and some alien force is pulling the strings. Someone or something that likes to see you squirm. It happens every month: the swelling and heaviness, the continual irritation of PMS. Nor is it any different for men, except that they usually haven't worked out the calendar. War is menstruation envy. In any case, male or female, you have no choice in the matter. They "offer you a body forever. To shit forever" (Burroughs). It's an offer you can't refuse; you simply have to breathe, eat, piss, shit, bleed, fuck, forever.

It's become fashionable to think that new computer technologies, or new interactive paradigms of mind, can somehow offer us a way out of this dilemma. Don't believe it for a second. Virtual reality is no gateway to transcendence. Consider the plight of the cyberspace "cowboys" in William Gibson's *Neuromancer*. They disdain the body, contemptuously dismissing it as "meat"; but they gradually learn that computerization doesn't release them from the flesh and its imperious demands. Cyberspace is ostensibly designed as a convenient, disembodied, and harmlessly neutral image of the world's amassed "information." But in fact the Matrix is anything but neutral; it bites and it kills. It is permeated by all sorts of strange forces: self-organizing alien interests, concentrations of political and economic power, irreducibly subjective kinks and quirks, remnants of genetic manipulations gone awry. As you ride through those "bright lattices of logic unfolding across that colorless void," you feel "an almost permanent adrenaline high," a corporeal kick as visceral and intense—and as compulsively addictive—as any sexual thrill or amphetamine rush. "Logic" and "information" stimulate specific physical circuits in the brain, just as drugs and panic attacks do. A wrong move, a neural overload, can be fatal. Even hallucinations need to be embodied. As all good AI researchers know, the software of the human mind has evolved and received its imprint from a particular configuration of neural hardware. You might have a brain based on silicon instead of carbon, but you can't do without some sort of physical organ. Your body accompanies you wherever you go: you can run, but you can't hide. Free your mind, and your ass will most certainly follow. In Gibson's corporate-controlled virtual space, as in the world of Cronenberg's *Videodrome*, "the visions become flesh, uncontrollable flesh." Images are incarnated as they are processed by the brain: fed back, via numerous reentrant loops, through the lateral geniculate nucleus, to the various subdivisions of the visual cortex. Synaptic connections grow as neurons are fired in self-reinforcing patterns. You tell yourself it's no big deal, that you can always stop if you want to, turn off the TV, jack out of the Matrix. Until one day you realize that you can't give it up after all, that you're trapped forever. You've become addicted to virtual reality, physiologically dependent upon those very images that seemed to promise you freedom from the flesh.

No, I'm not suggesting that you check into some 12-step program. Resist those insidious demands to testify and confess, proclaim your helplessness before the world, and parade your pain for others' delectation. It's more a question of neurophysiology than of psychology. In all forms of addiction, Gerald Fischbach tells us, "the nucleus accumbens, a small subdivision of the basal ganglia, appears to be particularly important." Short of surgical excision of this region, how could you ever escape being addicted to **CAPITAL**, or to **LIFE**? Remember Burroughs' formulations of the "algebra of need." Postmodern human beings need images, just as junkies need heroin, just as all mammals need oxygen to breathe. Tolerance increases as time goes by: you require ever more images, ever more stimuli, ever more intensive extractions of surplus value, merely for your body to survive in its excited or narcotized state. You must run faster and faster, like the Red Queen, just to stay in the same place. It's the law of the jungle, or more accurately of the free market: nobody can afford to relax, to slow down, to let go even for a second. One slight lapse, and you're out of the running forever, condemned to the endless, excruciating pains of withdrawal, bankruptcy, or extinction. DNA potentially replicates itself to infinity; but only if it has a suitable milieu to appropriate and exploit. Francesco Varela discusses the "structural coupling" and "codetermination" between organism and environment. No being is an island; every genome has what Richard Dawkins calls extended phenotypic effects. Sometimes these symbiotic exchanges are beneficial to all parties. But much more often, they lead to co-dependency, monopolization, or parasitic exploitation. We should never forget the harshness of natural selection: that one in a million, as Burroughs puts it, is very good biologic odds. Every strand of DNA potentially immortal; but as Burroughs warns us, the drive for immortality is the very paradigm of addiction: "He is addicted to an immortality predicated on the mortality of others . . . He needs your pain your fear your piss your human body that will die and keep him alive."

The heroes of **DOOM PATROL** meet just such an immortality addict: a strange being called Red Jack—he looks like the Jack of Hearts in a pack of playing cards—who claims to be both Jack the Ripper and God. (Grant Morrison appropriated him, I believe, from an episode of *Star Trek*). What link could there be between the creation of the universe and the serial killing of prostitutes? Both actions are exertions of power that turn out to involve a sullying Fall into materiality, or more precisely into the abject, addictive dependencies of the flesh. Red Jack spends most of his time querulously complaining about the injustices of his fate: "It's an old, old story. I created the universe, and they told me I had to be punished. Punished! And all because I had stained the beauty of perfect nothingness with gross matter." His murders follow a similar pattern: he wants to "cut up" women in order to "create a beautiful new form of life, something better than human"; but he ends up just making a terrible, gory mess. These accounts clearly identify Red Jack as what Gnostic theology would call an Archon: one of those lesser gods who rule over our prison universe of regimentation and suffering. Archons are like failed, untalented artists: their lust for power is never satiated, and their would-be acts of creativity are always botched. They are the ones who scared us all into time, into body, into shit. They made our flesh, and now they can't get along without it—and alas, neither can we. We are addicted to the nutriment and the pleasures they provide us, and they are addicted to the pungent flavors of our meat. Even the human nervous system, with its complex sensibility and its seemingly limitless capacity for self-deception, can't argue its way out of this vicious circle. You can go to as many recovery and support groups as you like, but all you'll be doing is exchanging one form of addiction for another.

The Marquis de Sade—whose materialist anti-theology often verges upon the Gnostic—argues that one's own pleasure is necessarily dependent upon the pain of others. All subjective experience is an epiphenomenal consequence of the motions and metamorphoses of matter; the intensity of my orgasm is directly proportional to the degree of agitation I can provoke and observe in the bodies of my victims. Pain is thus the original form of surplus value. Marx's theory of exploitation is yet another Gnostic account of our Fall into base matter—in this case, the commodity as fetish—and of the suffering that results therefrom. Nietzsche, still more clearly, sees pain as a primordial means of payment, as the oldest and most efficacious way of discharging one's debts. And so Red Jack literally feeds upon the surplus value of pain: he consumes the agony of millions of tortured butterflies, "pretty, fragile things with wings like church windows," pinned alive against the walls of his Baroque palace, shrieking in a music of perpetual torment. In Red Jack's nightmarish realm, "nothing actually dies. Here, there is only suffering. Pain sustains my existence." Flesh must be made to suffer, if it is to yield any sustenance, any substantial meaning. This is also the excuse for his career as Jack the Ripper. Beauty —in women or in butterflies—is a strange and delicate thing: subtle, transitory, and ultimately gratuitous. Its contingency is a threat to the solidity of male existence. That's why Plato banished poets from the city; that's why Heidegger joined the Nazi party. Red Jack similarly strives to wrest some sort of significance from a long history of errors, miscalculations, and random movements. There's no end to the suffering that we will impose— first on others, but finally on ourselves—in order to produce meaning and truth. "Man would rather will *nothingness*, than *not* will," as Nietzsche said. Red Jack expires when he can no longer sustain this project: when he realizes that his creations have been failures, that even pain is arbitrary and contingent, that "some stories have no meaning."

Despite the wishes of our rulers, our priests, and our philosophers, there's no ulterior source of value, nothing beyond this fragile lump of flesh. Energy is the only life, and is from the body: isn't that the scariest thing of all? The vulgar vitality of the flesh—and thence also its exquisite sensitivity, its capacity for limitless suffering—never seems to be depleted. No matter how many outrages Sade's libertines perpetrate upon the body of Justine, she always survives, virginal innocence intact, ready to be violated yet again. She is weak, infinitely weak; but her very vulnerability is what makes her inaccessible and indestructible within. Sade therefore argues that murder cannot be considered a crime, since strictly speaking it is impossible. For nothing is ever truly annihilated. Matter itself—today we should rather say mass-energy—is always precisely conserved; it can neither be created nor destroyed. With the full force of Enlightenment rationality, Sade argues for a thoroughgoing materialism. The true transmigration is one of bodies, not of souls. So all that you do when you kill somebody, Sade claims, is slightly to rearrange the atoms in certain minor molecular structures. And where's the iniquity in that?

Sade's greatness lies in his reiterated demonstrations that reason is the slave of the body and its passions. Philosophical argumentation, with the strictest logical rigor, can be derived from any premises whatsoever, and can be made to arrive at any arbitrarily desired conclusion. Nothing is true, everything is permitted. Sade invents a perfect alibi for murder—but at the price of banalizing the very act of murder, and rendering it utterly futile. For if everything is permitted, if there is no divine order to outrage and to violate, if killing is already Nature's customary way, then transgression is radically impossible. In proving so triumphantly that homicide is not a crime, Sade ruins his own pleasure in committing one. The real indignity of murder, from the libertine's point of view, lies in its ultimate impotence. For it always falls short of its goal: it never really attains its victim, it is never noxious and destructive enough. No amount of carnage is sufficient to compromise Justine's purity, or to remove her from the face of the earth. The more you make her suffer, the more powerfully you evince the dumb weight of her body's resistance. The mind can easily be colonized and controlled, but the flesh still endures. Sade's writing displays the sterile force of an addiction, with its obsessive repetitions and endless elaborations. For Sade can never exhaust the infinite perseverance of the flesh, never entirely subjugate it to the force of his will. A certain opaque carnality marks the absolute limit of his project of domination and transgression, which is to say of Enlightenment rationality itself.

That's why what's buried always returns: even if hideously decayed, and even if only in bits and pieces. The flesh is more than willing, though the spirit is all too weak. The "afterlife" is a wholly material phenomenon: it concerns the body, and not the soul. Today we fear the subsistence of the flesh, more than we do its annihilation. The great terror in George Romero's "living dead" trilogy is not being killed, but being unable to stay dead, being compelled to return as one of *them*. Postmodern space swarms with the Undead. Zombies throng our city danger zones, our suburban backyards, our shopping malls. Slashers in hockey masks, wielding chainsaws, rise up again and again. Organs and body parts pulse with an alien energy, and turn viciously against their owners: your own arm may try to strangle you, or knock you out with a sucker punch, as almost happens to Bruce Campbell in Sam Raimi's *Evil Dead II*. Raimi's and Romero's heroes face the classic problem in dealing with zombies: how do you kill something that's already dead? It's nearly impossible to be rid of them. You can show them out the front door, but they'll just come in again through the kitchen. You can cut them up into little bits, but they will reassemble in new configurations. Perhaps you can pulverize them in a food processor; but even this won't work, unless the parts are ground exceeding fine. The hero of Peter Jackson's *Dead Alive* (*Braindead*) is painfully lacking in social skills; he can't find a polite way to get his dead mother and other zombie guests to leave the house. Instead, he's forced to keep them locked in the basement, sedated on a steady diet of horse tranquilizers. He scrupulously feeds them himself, even pouring hot gruel directly into the gullet of one zombie who died of a slash to the throat. But he can't watch over their behavior every moment, and soon enough he finds that Mom has been naughty, and has given birth to a snarling, flesh-eating baby half-brother . . ..

We think that death is the end; but actually it's the failure to die—the vitality that subsists even in movements of decay and decomposition—that is fatal and irreversible. The worms crawl in, the worms crawl out. Even a nuclear holocaust would not much alter the ecological balance of the planet: the world would still be dominated, as it is now, by insects and bacteria. The afterlife is not a fixed state, but a process of slow contagion, insidiously, inexorably spreading. In Brian Yuzna's *Bride of Reanimator*, reanimation fluid accidentally seeps into the water table, and ends up reviving corpses in a nearby cemetery. This is not immortality, but its sinister parody: a grotesque hyperbole of mortality and finitude. It's bad enough when living people get turned into zombies, but even worse when dead people do too. For these beings aren't granted anything like eternal life. Their deprivation is rather raised to a bizarre higher power: they lose not only the ability to live, but also the ability to die. Their fate, like that of Red Jack's victims, has been shorn of its supposed meaning; it no longer displays that sanctimonious aura of tragic inevitability. "The finite world suggests a contingency to the second power that does not found any freedom: It *is capable of not not-being*, it is capable of the irreparable ... The Irreparable is that things are just as they are, in this or that mode, consigned without remedy to their way of being" (Giorgio Agamben).

That's why it's high time "to have done with the judgment of God." There is no higher necessity in the fact of these bodies having been slashed to ribbons, or of these walking dead having become what they now are. There is no inexorable movement of fate and retribution. There's only a brutal process of natural selection, without any preordained goal. Evolution can lead to adaptive improvements; but no teleology is involved, and no possibility of transcendence. These actions are irreparable; "an evolutionary step that involves mutation is irretrievable and irreversible" (Burroughs). You can deny the body only by means of the body; you can escape death only by invoking death. It's easy enough to kill somebody, but extraordinarily difficult to dispose of the remains. Capital punishment only ends up repeating and amplifying the crime it is supposed to punish. And suicide is still more pointless, because it's only a temporary solution to a permanent and ever-recurring problem. You can choose to initiate such mortal processes, but they will always spiral out of your control. Nobody, Burroughs says, can "hire DEATH as a company cop." Death is like debt, as when an S&L issues junk bonds. You live off a debt or a death that is always continually increasing, but that is also indefinitely deferred. But however long you avoid paying off your loans, the debt or death will never be definitively cancelled. Capitalizing on pain just lowers the threshold of your addiction, and increases the size of your long-term payments. Postponing the end also means prolonging the agony. The more you seek to deny or transcend mortality, the more you ironically intensify its thrills and terrors. The more you distance yourself from your flesh, the more that flesh is made vulnerable. Just when you thought it was safe to go back into the water, you discover that you've contracted some vile infection, or become susceptible to the tremors of unwelcome arousal. No Buddhist detachment is possible: no stepping off the wheel of karma, no escape from the food chain. Anyplace, anytime, you are prone to be convulsed yet again in what Karen Finley calls "the constant state of desire . . . the fear of living, as opposed to the fear of dying."

Postmodern horror most commonly appears as a farcical theater of blood—without the pomposity of tragedy, without the facile consolations of myth. Contemporary taste rightly prefers *Titus Andronicus* to *King Lear*. There's no culmination, no conclusion, no catharsis; but only slow adaptive changes in the nature of the media, and in the technology of special effects. Who wants to see a woman cut in two with an old-fashioned handsaw, asks the gleefully sarcastic magician in Herschell Gordon Lewis' *The Wizard of Gore*, when now we have at our disposal such tools as electric drills, pile drivers, and chainsaws? The Wizard's magic is just a matter of film editing: shots of women being mutilated by such tools are intercut with shots of them surviving unharmed. Members of the hypnotized audience are all too ready to offer themselves up to the Wizard's cynical experiments—though usually it's the boys who persuade or force their girlfriends to subject themselves to these tortures. The magic show over, the women return safely to their seats; but their dead and mangled bodies are discovered shortly thereafter. Lewis once remarked in an interview that he'd gladly have men as well as women sliced up in his films, if only he could find a large enough audience willing to pay for such a spectacle. But who's to argue with popular taste? Lewis has a sharp eye for what the market will bear, in terms of gruesomeness and gore: which explains the history of his career changes, from English professor to exploitation film maker to direct mail marketing consultant. As Lewis understands, there's always something jovial and festive—carnivalesque, Bakhtin would say—about watching horror films, just as there used to be about attending public executions and tortures. (Walter Kendrick's fine book, *The Thrill of Fear*, provides a history of these entertainments). Gore flicks, with their campy excesses and gratuitously elaborated special effects, are a mode of expenditure particularly suited to our postmodern world of visceral illusions and interactive electronic media. *The Wizard of Gore* merely pushes this logic to its radical extreme: the wizard goes on TV to present his theater of universal cruelty, in which each and every member of the home viewing audience is invited to participate, both as distracted spectator and as mutilated victim.

The Marquis de Sade campaigned passionately against the death penalty, being unable to countenance its cruelty. But things have changed in the last two hundred years. Today, we complain because the executions of killers like Gary Gilmore, Ted Bundy, and Wesley Dodd aren't shown live on TV. One Republican legislator in my state went so far as to demand that Dodd's hanging take place with his victims' relatives present, since it was "a family event, like a baptism or a marriage." These enthusiastic supporters of capital punishment are of course the same people who want to ban abortion, and who worry about excessive sex and violence in movies and pop music. They seek to keep the body's aberrations and addictions in control, under reserve, as the sole prerogative of the patriarchal nuclear family and of the repressive State. On the contrary, when zombies are on the loose, or when the Wizard of Gore broadcasts his bloody illusions on TV, at least we can be damn sure that the Republicans will also get theirs. Horror films overturn established values, for they celebrate whatever is arbitrary, irresponsible, irreparable, transitory, and contingent. They gleefully exploit—for public delectation and for private profit—the fragility and vulnerability, and yet the infinite, inhuman perdurability, of this meat, this body, this suffering flesh.

6. CLIFF STEELE

William Burroughs writes: "in this life we have to take things as we find them as the torso murderer said when he discovered his victim was a quadruple amputee." Good advice for the anatomically deranged, like **DOOM PATROL**'s Cliff Steele. Cliff has a problem with his body, you see. It happened like this. He used to be a daredevil racing car driver; he had a horrible wreck. Nearly all of him was burned to ashes, but they snatched his brain from the flames. And then they implanted that brain in a new prosthetic body, all shiny metal, ultra high tech, a veritable fighting machine. Now Cliff is the muscle of the **DOOM PATROL**, a brain turned into brawn. They expect him to be a macho bruiser, when actually he's quite sensitive underneath. And to add insult to injury, they call him Robotman—a name he violently hates. What would that do for your sense of self-esteem? The life of a superhero these days! Cliff thinks of himself as just a regular guy; Robocop fantasies are the last thing on his mind. But with a metallic casing like this, he can't exactly blend into the crowd. It's what Baudrillard calls *hypervisibility*, the postmodern condition par excellence. No chance of chilling out with a secret identity, like old Clark Kent used to do. All this metal is a clunky encumbrance, no matter how great its tensile strength. You know you're in bad shape when you bang your head against a wall, and you still don't feel a thing. At this point, Cliff doesn't even really know what his body can do. How good is all this cyber-tech stuff anyway? How accurate and detailed is sensory input? How fast is motor response? What unaccustomed relays and connections now trigger the pain and pleasure centers in Cliff's brain? Will he ever be able to taste and smell? Can he ever have sex again? What about getting drunk or stoned? "The only good thing about having a human brain in a robot body," Cliff remarks sardonically at one point, "is that it's easier to control brain chemistry." Just the touch of a button, and anxiety is dissipated, alertness is heightened, or memory is enhanced. But alas, this techno-manipulability has been wired to work only for utilitarian ends, not hedonistic ones.

"Our machines are disturbingly lively," Donna Haraway writes, "and we ourselves frighteningly inert." It might not be so bad, if only you could get used to the situation. After all, Descartes argued long ago that the body is a machine. It shouldn't matter all that much whether metal or flesh is the material. In either case, it's simply a matter of mastering the electro-chemical interface: regularizing chains of association, facilitating neural feedback patterns, reinforcing the appropriate reentrant connections. In short, a question of recognition and memory, of cultivating habits over the course of time. The problem is that Cliff's mechanical body never stays the same. He's continually being sent back to the shop for upgrades and repairs. Transistors burn out; programming errors and faulty couplings throw him off stride. He gets into fights, and enemies regularly mangle his metal to bits. And if that wasn't bad enough, Doc Magnus (who built and programmed his body in the first place) and Niles Caulder (the Chief of the **DOOM PATROL**) tend to use Cliff as a pawn in their ongoing professional rivalry. Neither of them is content to let well enough alone; they are both all too eager to retool Cliff in order to try out their latest cybernetic design ideas. And let's not even think about those insectoid aliens who at one point fit Cliff out in a new metal carapace with six legs. Life in a robot body, even if you're strong, is just one humiliation after another. The persistence of memory in the brain only makes things worse. Amputees typically feel phantom sensations in their lost limbs; poor Cliff has this problem multiplied many times over. He endlessly relives numerous episodes of mutilation and dismemberment. Neither Clint Eastwood nor Woody Allen—our two best-known icons of hetero-male angst— ever had to go through anything remotely like this.

The worst part, though, is the waiting. All these body modifications take time, just as it takes time to alter a dress or a pair of pants. Cliff's brain is disconnected meanwhile, and left in a vat of nutrient fluids. The experience isn't exactly like returning to the womb. You don't get some soothing "oceanic feeling"; rather, you freak out from sensory deprivation. The first stage is "boredom: hearing nothing, seeing nothing, experiencing nothing. Boredom and irritation and then panic." Panic, because the brain (like nature) abhors a vacuum. So that's when the hallucinations begin: "nightmares of sound and vision, grotesque sensory distortions." Cliff is overwhelmed by paranoid delusions of a world controlled by malevolent insects and soulless infernal machines. "The body becomes remote, robotic, disconnected," a symptom of the schizophrenic's "sense of being abstracted from the day-to-day physical world." But if this is the case with me, then what about other people? "Maybe I'm not the robot, and everyone else is." It doesn't help to realize that this is just a virtual world, and that your own brain is generating all these visions. If anything, such an awareness only makes things worse: your ontological insecurity is heightened, while the horrors you confront don't for all that become any less vivid and intense. If only I could attribute these appearances to a malevolent programmer, to somebody like Descartes' evil demon! Then at least I'd have the comfort of knowing that somebody else is out there, that I'm not absolutely alone. True hell for Cliff is the solipsistic universe of Bishop Berkeley, in which nothing exists except one's own inner perceptions: a closed circle from which there is no escape.

But fortunately this idealist delirium doesn't last forever; eventually the hallucinations subside. Virtual reality is a great leveller: "nothing can pass through without being broken down, disintegrated." And so Cliff finally reaches a sort of nirvana, "something I can't describe: the center of the cyclone, the room without doors." Now becoming grinds to a halt; time no longer passes, you have all the time in the world. Plenty of time to meditate upon the Smiths lyric that opens and closes one episode of **DOOM PATROL**: "Does the body rule the mind or does the mind rule the body?" The question resonates in the emptiness like a Zen koan: ironic, unanswerable, absurd. Meditate long enough, and the inner self, the first person of the Cartesian *cogito*, drops out of the picture. You're left with the great postmodern discovery, anticipated alike by Hume and by the Buddhists: that personal identity is a fiction. The Cartesian subject disappears, together with all that it created. When I introspect deeply, I may come across all sorts of experiential contents and structures: feelings, desires, perceptions, memories, multiple personalities, and so on. But the one thing I am absolutely unable to find is *myself*.

The conundrum of the brain in a vat is an old philosophical slapstick routine, an updated postmodern version of Descartes' original *Meditations*. The question is always the same: how can I know *for sure* that these inner representations correspond to something out there, that what I experience is real? How can I be *absolutely certain* that I'm not just a disembodied mind dreaming the external world, or that it isn't all a computer simulation fed into my brain by direct innervation of the neuronal fibers? The comedy lies in this: that it's only my hysterical demand for certainty that first introduces the element of doubt. It's only by subjecting myself to the horrors of sensory deprivation that I approach the delirious limit at which the senses become questionable. Descartes does just that in his *Third Meditation*: "I will now shut my eyes, stop my ears, and withdraw all my senses . . ." Descartes "proves God," as Samuel Beckett puts it, "by exhaustion." As metaphysics goes, it's the oldest trick in the book: first you take something away, then you complain that it isn't there, and then you invent a theory grounded in—and compensating for—its very absence. Deleuze and Guattari call it the Theology of Lack. A seductive ruse, to be sure: once you accept the premises, you've already been suckered into the conclusions.

"If I only had a brain . . ." For as one character in **DOOM PATROL** remarks, "Descartes was nothing but a miserable git who never had a good time in his entire life!" Postmodern philosophers rightly reject the very logic that gets us into the dualist impasse. Descartes' methodical doubt is ultimately a distinction without a difference, since it has no pragmatic consequences whatsoever. For consider the alternatives. Either there's some telltale sign, which allows me to empirically determine whether or not I am just a brain kept in a vat: in which case the whole sorry mess is merely a question of fact, without any deeper epistemological import. Or else, there's no way of telling: but in this case, I have nothing to worry about, since my experience will remain the same one way or the other. "The mystery," as Cormac McCarthy's Judge Holden says, "is that there is no mystery." Perhaps the evil demon posited by Descartes gets some private, masturbatory delectation out of fooling us like this; but that needn't be any concern of ours. For the evil demon can't *do* anything to us, can't harm us or change us or otherwise affect us, without thereby tipping his hand and revealing his existence. Descartes' dilemma is resolved without dualism,and without positing a transcendent self, simply by noting that appearances and simulacra are themselves perfectly real. The *cogito* is reduced to a third-person tautology: things are exactly as they are and what they are. In this postmodern life, "we have to take things as we find them."

But such logic and such consolations are of little help to Cliff Steele, trapped as he is in all that heavy metal—except for the even worse times when his naked brain is actually left to stew and hallucinate in a vat. If modern Western rationality begins with Descartes' willfully self-mutilating gesture, perhaps it culminates in Cliff's absurd disembodiment. Cliff is the final, helpless, involuntary victim of a whole history of amputations. He is compelled *literally* to live out the disabling paradoxes of Cartesian dualism. He suffers every day from schizophrenic disjunctions between the real and the imaginary, between self and other, between vitalism and mechanism, between mind and body. The problem may be a false one philosophically, but it's still inscribed in our technology. Descartes' idle speculations are now as it were incised in Cliff's very flesh. Doc Magnus and the Chief mess with Cliff's head more insidiously than the evil demon ever could. Their operations give dualism a delirious new twist: for now it's Cliff's mind that is materially incarnated, while his corporeality is entirely notional, virtual, and simulacral. Such is our postmodern refinement of those old metaphysical endeavors to find the ultimate reality, to separate essence from accident. Descartes' *cogito* and Husserl's *epoche* were merely thought experiments; but now we can realize their equivalents in actual surgical procedures. Strip everything away that is not indubitably "Cliff Steele," that is not necessarily contained in the very notion of his essence; and what's left is precisely these three pounds of neuronal tissue, a fleshy lump "so full of water that it tends to slump like a blancmange if placed without support on a firm surface" (Anthony Smith, *The Body*). Since Cliff's only 'identity' is that of this actual, physical brain, you might say that his sole grounding certitude is that he is an extended thing—as against Descartes' claim to be a thinking thing. Just as you can't make an omelette without breaking eggs—as 60s revolutionaries used to say—so you can't get amputated unless you have a body.

The Chief claims that the operation was a success, that it's all turned out for Cliff's own greater good. The old Cliff Steele, he says, was "selfish, arrogant, overconfident, ill-educated ... a loudmouthed, misogynistic boor"; it's only through the traumas of amputation and cyborgization that the new Cliff "learn[s] kindness and compassion and a selfless heroism." **DOOM PATROL** is quite different from the revisionist superhero comics that made a big splash in the mid to late 80s: Alan Moore's and Dave Gibbons' *Watchmen*, Frank Miller's *Batman: The Dark Knight Returns* (with Klaus Janson and Lynn Varley), and Grant Morrison's own *Batman: Arkham Asylum* (with Dave McKean). All these works 'deconstruct' our familiar images of comic book superheroes. They go behind the scenes to reveal what we should've suspected all along: that Batman and all those other patriotic, costumed crime-fighters are really violent sociopaths with fascist-cum-messianic leanings and a kinky underwear fetish. Everything gets played out for these sordid characters in the registers of secrecy, disguise, and paranoia: literally in the form of their jealous anxieties about maintaining a "secret identity," and more figuratively in terms of those notorious paradoxes of destroying the world in order to save it, or stepping outside of the law in order to enforce the law. As the elder Mayor Daley of Chicago once said, "the police are not there to create disorder; the police are there to preserve disorder." Miller's Batman and Moore's tormented antiheroes owe much to the creepy affectlessness and suppressed fury of Clint Eastwood's Dirty Harry. Indeed, their hoods and masks go Clint one better, when it comes to maintaining an unreadable, deadpan exterior. The crime-fighter's costume is a literal "character armor," rigidly neutralizing whatever may rage beneath—and thereby perpetuating the modernist fantasy that there is a "beneath," something like manhood or interiority or selfhood.

Most of these psychotic superheroes are still organically human; but it's only one more step to outright androids and cyborgs, like Arnold Schwarzenegger's Terminator and Peter Weller's Robocop (in fact, Frank Miller worked on the scripts for *Robocop II* and *III*). And hasn't there always been something cyborg-like about Clint? In the cyborg fantasy films, in any case, the superhero's costume—I include Arnold's muscles in this category—no longer works as a disguise. Now it's a prosthetic organ of strength, a kind of supplemental, rebuilt manhood. Todd McFarlane's comic book *Spawn* (a series to which Alan Moore and Grant Morrison have both contributed) presents an even more fascinating case. Here, the protagonist's costume is not just an article of clothing, nor even a mechanical interface, but a living inhuman being in its own right: a sexually voracious, "constantly-evolving neural parasite" from Hell that brings Al Simmons back from the dead, heightens his metabolism, encases him in an unbreachable protective carapace, and takes command of his central nervous system. The image is definitely insect-like: hard armor on the outside, guarding some soft squishy stuff within. Al's body is nearly invulnerable; but this security only intensifies his hidden anguish. He wallows in the misery of living in back alleys with the homeless, while mourning the loss of his wife and child, to whom he can never return. And so Al gets to display his macho prowess, while at the same time laying claim to a deep inner sensitivity, a self-righteous feeling of vulnerability and victimization. Can Robert Bly and his "men's movement" be far behind? Again and again it's the same old story: a near-catatonic rigidity that is breached only in outbursts of extreme cathartic violence, whether by banging drums in the woods, or by blowing away the slavering hordes of sickos and scumbags with a .357 Magnum. At least Clint has a keen sense of irony about it all—which is more than you can say for Bly or McFarlane or Woody Allen. Some guys'll do anything to redeem their lonely, frustrated lives. And so they endow their experience with a certain self-aggrandizing pathos, by entertaining reactive, resentful fantasies of masculinity under siege. It feels so good to be a victim, because then you've got the perfect excuse to demand recompense, to make others pay like you've had to pay, to lash out at the bitch who started it all.

A man's gotta do what a man's gotta do. You imagine your 'manhood' as something both strong and fragile, hard and tough and yet continually in peril. Like a penis that might go limp, or a mind weighted down with a body. But why even bother, why hold back? Why not just let yourself go? Why cling to this rigid exterior armor, why nurture this aggrieved inner self? Can Cartesian dignity mean that much to you? OK, OK, you'll say—together with Descartes and with Arnold—this body is only a machine, but there's still something inside that's really *me*. I had to destroy my cock in order to save it: I tore it apart and had it recast in hard, cutting metal—a strategy implicit in many of these comic books and films, and savagely literalized in Shinya Tsukamoto's *Iron Man*. Marshall McLuhan describes techno-hysteria as a defensive reaction to change, "a desperate and suicidal autoamputation, as if the central nervous system could no longer depend on the physical organs to be protective buffers against the slings and arrows of outrageous mechanism." But McLuhan also insists that there's no backing away from the dilemma: "there is, for example, no way of refusing to comply with the new sense ratios or sense 'closure' evoked by the TV image." It isn't a question of adapting ourselves to a new technological environment, but of realizing that this technology already *is* our adaptation. We must cultivate the new sensations offered to us by our new organs. And if masculinity can't keep up with the changes, then so much the worse for masculinity.

Grant Morrison understands these dynamics better than anyone. His *Batman: Arkham Asylum* pushes the revisionist superhero comic to a parodic point of no return. Batman's old enemies, now inmates of the asylum for the criminally insane, tauntingly invite him to join them. For isn't the 'virtual' freedom of madness more appealing than the tedium of life in the 'real' world, "confined to the Euclidean prison that is sanity"? Batman is all too receptive to such a seduction. He knows he's as crazy as any of them, what with his bizarre fixations and his hysterical rage for order. He senses that walking through the doors of Arkham Asylum will be "just like coming home." And indeed, once he arrives, the blood of self-mutilation flows unchecked. Virility crumbles in an onslaught of psychedelic dislocation. The Cartesian fiction of the mind as a faithful "mirror of nature" (as Richard Rorty calls it) is shattered and scattered into the multiple grotesque reflections of the Asylum's funhouse mirrors. The Joker captures Batman, but declines to unmask him and reveal his secret identity; for he knows that the Caped Crusader's mask already "is his real face." I've loved the Joker ever since I was a child, so I was thrilled by Morrison's reinvention of his character. The Joker may well be a gleefully sadistic mass murderer, but he's also an exemplary postmodern subject. For he "has no real personality; he creates himself each day. He sees himself as the Lord of Misrule, and the world as a theatre of the absurd." The Joker responds to the "chaotic barrage" of his overloaded senses—the postmodern information glut—in a radically new manner. Not by choosing and discriminating among his perceptions; and not by striving to maintain a fixed ego structure. But simply by "going with the flow"; he immerses himself in the postmodern flux and just lets it all happen. Unlike Batman, the Joker no longer needs the "protective buffers" that McLuhan feared were numbing us to change. He knows that the only way out is first of all a way in and through. His great adaptive innovation is to hold nothing back; he *lives* and *enjoys* the postmodern condition, this mutation of our sensibility into non-linear, non-Euclidean forms. Far from being mad, the Joker may in fact represent "some kind of super-sanity . . . a brilliant new modification of human perception, more suited to urban life at the end of the twentieth century."

The Joker's difference from Batman parallels McLuhan's distinction between *hot* and *cool* media. "A hot medium," McLuhan says, "is one that extends *one single sense* in 'high definition.'" Its chief characteristics are "homogeneity, uniformity, and linear continuity." Hot media are imperious, unidirectional, even terroristic. They demand rapt contemplation or close, obsessive attentiveness. Your life at every second depends upon their dictates, and yet they leave you feeling strangely uninvolved. They keep you at a proper, 'alienated' distance, drawing you into a paranoid frenzy of endless interpretation. This is the culture of the Book: of fundamentalist Christians scrutinizing their Bibles, and of academics "reading" the insidious ideologies embedded in the seemingly innocuous practices of everyday life. Batman is a quintessentially *hot* figure, ever on the lookout for whatever minuscule clues will confirm his Manichean sense of the world's depravity. Cool media, on the other hand, are 'low-definition,' and for that very reason "high in participation or completion by the audience." Their sparse spaces welcome and envelop us. They are characterized by "pluralism, uniqueness, and discontinuity," and they solicit high levels of feedback and involvement. A cool medium, McLuhan says in a famous pun, offers you a *massage* rather than a *message*: a multi-textured, tactile and sensual experience, rather than the rational finality of a meaning to be decoded. There is nothing to interpret. Instead, cool media invite the kind of open reception that Michael Taussig, elaborating on Walter Benjamin, calls *distraction*: "a very different apperceptive mode, a type of flitting and barely conscious peripheral visual perception." This is the Joker's random drift, a delirious passivity brilliantly adapted to our state of continual technological shock. With innovation running at so fast a pace, alienation is out of date. It's no longer a case of me against the world. Contrary to the overwrought claims of high-minded media pundits, nobody's ever been brainwashed by watching TV. In fact, most people talk back to their sets. As Clark Humphrey puts it, "people who consume lots of media are *very* cynical about what they're consuming . . . A typical nonviewer may believe almost anything, [but] a typical TV viewer treats everything with (excess?) skepticism." Our cheerful postmodern skepticism—reacting as if everything were just "on TV," or always already in quotation marks—is poles apart from modernist angst or from Cartesian methodical doubt. You can't ever defeat the evil demon in open battle, but you can put him in his place once you realize that he has more in common with Chuck Barris and Maury Povich than he does with Satan or God.

You might say that when Cliff Steele lost everything except for his brain, he was thrust willy-nilly into this cool new postmodern world. With all his "protective buffers" gone, he was 'preadapted' to change. He had no choice but to be plugged directly into the "extension of the central nervous system" that electronic media have made of our planet. The Chief is right: something inside Cliff has been altered forever, so there's no point in even trying to recover what was lost. "We have to take things as we find them," amputations and all. This is "what it's like" to be a postmodern cyborg. Prosthetic surgery is painful, but it can powerfully renew our sense of involvement in the world. It's all a question of where you locate the information interface: how much you can stand to lop off, or just how far back you're willing to go. Daniel Dennett notes that the question of the interface is the fatal weak point of every mind/body dualism: how can something be wholly immaterial, and yet still have material effects? Descartes placed the transfer point in the pineal gland; phenomenologists extend it to the surface of the skin; spiritualists push it even further out, to the ectoplasmic aura that surrounds us like a crustacean carapace or a superhero's sheath. But for Cliff it no longer makes sense even to draw the line. Neurons and wires are much the same stuff. The electrochemical feedback loops that constitute Cliff's brain are of the same nature as those that are wired into his prosthetic body, or that course across the entirety of the postmodern "global village." Cliff's feelings, like the ashes of his former body, are scattered more or less everywhere. But there's no *one single point* at which the experiences become "his own."

So in this strange way, Cliff is the postmodern Everyman. He hasn't quite been 'feminized,' but at least he's no "misogynistic boor." It's true he suffers from a certain baffled frustration, from a perpetual sense of unfulfilled duty, from frequent bouts of self-pity, and from a chronic inability to relax. Nothing seems vital to Cliff any more; as his psychiatrist asks him at one point, "how must it feel to have saved a world you don't really believe is worth saving?" But unlike the old superheroes, Cliff doesn't feel any differently about the world than he does about himself. The distinction of inner and outer simply isn't relevant any more. That's why his pathos has nothing vengeful about it; it can't be seen as the reaction of a resentful masculine ego. This pathos is rather the very affect or quality of that ego's having been dispersed. It's the expression, not of Cliff's subjectivity, but precisely of his no longer being a "subject" in the old Cartesian/Freudian sense. It's the feeling of not *having* a center—but also of not even *lacking* one. A cool, prosthetic pathos, perfect for an age of television and computers. What is the ontological status of this "soul of a new machine," this deeply intimate, yet strangely unlocalizable, affect? Call it a secondary, sympathetic resonance; or an uneliminable redundancy; or an effect of multiple interference patterns; or an emergent property of information flows accelerated beyond a certain threshold. As Deleuze suggests, we need to replace the old phenomenological slogan ("all consciousness is consciousness *of* something") with a new, radically decentered one: "all consciousness is something." For this is what happens when your brain is plugged directly into the world's "mixing board" (Cronenberg); but also when it's isolated in a vat, or when its contents are downloaded into the VR matrix of a supercomputer. Round and round and round it goes; where it stops, nobody knows. "Does the body rule the mind or does the mind rule the body? I don't know." No *cogito*, then; no *ergo*, and no *sum*. "I don't know if the world is better or worse than it has been"—as Kathy Acker writes in a different context—"I know the only anguish comes from running away."

7. CINDY SHERMAN

The images implore us, seduce us, perhaps delude us. No mere verbal descriptions can do them justice. The woman sits in a window frame, low-cut blouse, hot pants, bobby sox, high heeled shoes, glancing out of the window with frustrated expectation, and perhaps also a hint of boredom. The woman, all in black, in semi-shadow, stands leaning by the fireplace, beneath a landscape painting, cigarette in one upraised hand, pensive. The woman lies on her back, head towards us, outstretched diagonally across a hotel bed, frilly white evening dress, pearl necklace, lost some-where between reverie and exhaustion. The woman sits at the table, empty drink glass in front of her, medium close-up, upper torso and face, black dress with leopard-skin neck and sleeves, tears streaming down her heavily made-up face.

How many times have we seen such scenes before? Cindy Sherman's black-and-white "Untitled Film Stills" (1977-1980) teeter on the brink between cliché and revelation. Overloaded with detail, these pictures are nonetheless fundamentally empty. Nothing is happening, although far too much has already happened or is about to happen. Present time has been drained of its vitality and fullness; it is no longer that living immediacy whose recovery is the utopian promise of every snapshot. Rather, the moment seems to have been emptied out: emaciated to the point where it is only the thinnest of membranes, barely separating a traumatic past from a fatal future. Each photograph is ostensibly a "self-portrait": Sherman casts herself in a series of clichéd roles from 40s and 50s low-budget melodramas and film noirs. These women are fragile, lonely, confused, abandoned, wistful, or timidly seductive: not glamorous drag queens like Mae West, Jean Harlow, and Marilyn Monroe, but humbler stereotypes of a traditional, depressed femininity. They are uncertain, indecisive, achingly passive and vulnerable, unable to act. All they can do is wait. Time is frozen. The film projector has jammed: this single frame, this insubstantial instant, one twenty-fourth of a second, will last forever. The women are caught in the time warp of their retro stylizations: they are defined and constrained by their postures, their make-up, their clothes, none of which will ever change. They are trapped in their images. For what is an image, after all? "A superb power," to quote Blanchot ironically quoting Pascal, "which makes eternity into nothingness and nothingness into eternity."

These women cannot really be called *individuals*, for everything about them is subordinated to the clichés of genre fiction, and to the standardized rules of feminine behavior. There are as many prosthetic female selves as there are different videotapes of old movies to rent, or different TV programs to watch. Which is why Sherman has to make so many different images, why her serial repetitions produce multiple sets of stereotypes, instead of fixing on just one. The women in the "Untitled Film Stills" are stereotypes, puppets, playing out their pre-assigned scripts. Their inner life is utterly blocked. They are so frail, so vulnerable. They need you, it seems, to complete their story. Save me. Protect me. Penetrate me. Possess me. And so virility rides to the rescue. But isn't that the biggest cliché of all? What's missing from this picture? You say that these women are suffering from "lack," so that you can be the one to fulfill and complete them. But it doesn't work.

You find that these images continually slip beyond your grasp, out of your possession. You can't get it up, you can't get the film projector up and running again, you can't supply the missing narratives that would release the trapped figures from their suspension. The stifling intimacy of these scenarios is such that there can be no referential 'real' in which to anchor them, and no Archimedean point from which to regard them. These images lure you instead into a paralysis as great as their own, into the realm of the unspeakable, the unsayable. This is what Blanchot calls the time of fascination: "the time of the absence of time, the time in which nothing begins, without negation, without decision, where before affirmation there is already the return of affirmation."

These women offer you no point of approach. You can't even really define them as recognizable 'types.' Their presence is too disturbingly indefinite for that. Their faces have congealed into sterile masks of anticipation, yearning, dread, fatigue, insecurity, or boredom. Wittgenstein suggests that such conditions should not be regarded as "mental states" at all. One isn't bored or sad or expectant in the same way that one is cold or hot, or that one suddenly feels a sharp pain, or that one sees colors and hears sounds. That is to say, affects like grief, longing, and exhaustion aren't really 'psychological,' since they are devoid of intentional and phenomenological content. Wittgenstein points out that we quite easily say: "For a second he felt violent pain"; but that it would "sound queer to say: 'For a second he felt deep grief.'" For "grief describes a pattern which recurs, with different variations, in the weave of our life," but which cannot be circumscribed as a particular mental activity. The "now" of all these emotions—the "now" of the figures in Sherman's photographs—is different from the "now" of sensation and comprehension. It's an oddly impersonal "now," without contours, without discernible limits, and without fixed location. These affects are everyday banalities, they are all perfectly real; only they aren't accessible to our usual powers of self-conscious introspection. They steal over me before I am aware of them, and somehow separate me from myself. They come over me in waves, breaking down my self-possession and self-control. They turn me into a stereotype, drained of interiority, emotionally unbalanced and strangely vulnerable. In short, they turn me into a woman.

But now consider another group of Sherman's photographs, this time in lurid, 'living' color: the "Untitled" series from 1992. Here Sherman is no longer content just to try on Mommy's old clothes; instead, she gleefully mixes and matches the stereotypical, prefabricated parts of "anatomically correct medical-supply-house dolls." Skin and fabric give way to plastic. These prosthetic "self-portraits" are no longer content to suffer passively: they are bloody, violent, predatory, dangerously unbalanced, obsessed with mutilation and disease. Faces are grotesquely masked, wrinkled with age, or distended in (orgasmic or agonizing?) screams. Enormous dolls, part female and part male, offer themselves to the camera in 'fuck-me' postures. Cunts gape open distended with blood and shit, or sprout monstrous erections from which ooze unhealthy fluids. Heads winch apart from their prosthetic torsos, and limbless trunks testify to torturous amputations. This aggressive fragmentation of the body frees organs and orifices from the tedious constraints of organic unity. Cunts, assholes, and breasts reek with infection, crying out desperately to be fondled, penetrated, or milked. These images are a threat—perhaps to the projections of female narcissism, and certainly to the anxious defensiveness of male pricks and egos. But they also carry the promise of strange and novel pleasures. Long live the new flesh. Sherman returns to the autopsy table and remakes human anatomy, just as Artaud demanded.

Vision itself is wounded and infected in these photographs: solicited, embodied, taken hostage, fragmented, shattered. Out, vile jelly. "What happens when what you see, even though from a distance, seems to touch you with a grasping contact, when the manner of seeing is a sort of touch, when seeing is *contact* at a distance? What happens when what is seen imposes itself on your gaze, as though the gaze had been seized, touched, put in contact with appearance?" (Blanchot). These images leave you no room for detached, disinterested contemplation. They draw you into the scenario, and make you feel sullied by the *touch* of ocular contact. Nobody can refuse to take part in *this* orgy. The merest glance, and it's already too late. How reductive of Freud to describe the fear of blindness, of "base matter" touching and tainting the eyes, as a derivative of castration anxiety. In such disarticulated and prosthetic flesh, there can be no hierarchy of the organs or the senses, no privileging of sight over touch or male over female, of cocks over cunts or cocks over eyes. Woman has sex organs more or less everywhere, as Luce Irigaray puts it, and as Doctor Schreber already knew. And in this postmodern delirium, we are all more or less women. A decentered, tactile, polymorphous economy of the flesh replaces the old phallic and visual one. Irigaray's evocation of the fluidity, intimacy, tactility, and volume of female bodies corresponds with Marshall McLuhan's apprehension of the tactile, synesthetic qualities of the new electronic media. Every tech- nological innovation, McLuhan says, implies a radical reordering of the human nervous system. Postmodern experience no longer conforms to the print-centered, phallocentric paradigm of a distanced, objectifying, linear, and perspectival vision. Now, in the age of video and computers, of genetic engineering and prosthetic surgery, the eye touches rather than sees; it immerses itself in the photograph, to be traversed by its erotic and emetic flows, and caressed and violated all along its surfaces.

So this is what it means to be a woman. Femininity, we now realize, is a variable construction, not a pre-given mythological essence. Ladies are made and not born. It's not enough just to have a cunt, or XX chromosomes, in order to become a woman. Genes can be spliced, and cunts, too, are prosthetically manufactured. But how, then, *are* women constructed? What are little girls made of? "Sugar and spice and everything nice" can be a difficult dish to swallow. It has to be mixed just right, or else it might make you queasy. It must flatter your nose and tickle your palate, melt pleasantly in your mouth and not in your hands, and soothe your throat as it slides smoothly down into your belly. Femininity is less an effect of language or ideology than it is the result of an actual labor upon the body. Adornment of the surfaces, and penetration into the depths. Hormone balances and cosmetic applications. A rigorous training in posture, gesture and dress. There's a curious ambiguity at the heart of this process, an insidious, fascinating slippage from obligation to desire, from coercion to seduction. I resent it, yet I become absorbed in it. I give way, now to vertiginous ecstasy, now to violent bursts of all-consuming rage. "Happiness in slavery," as Jean Paulhan describes the paradox of Pauline Réage's *Story of O*, the quintessential novel of feminine apprenticeship. It's an emotional push-and-pull so extreme, so slippery and unstable, that it can't just be called 'ambivalence.' For it's not that I am indecisively torn between different attitudes, so much as that I experience the full strength of incompatible affects at one and the same time. I feel it in my entrails, pushing ever deeper, churning up my insides. It's like being fist-fucked in the cunt and the asshole simultaneously, an intensity almost too great to bear: "they were practically holding hands inside her. Only a thin membrane kept them apart. She could feel them flexing their muscles, turning; even an eighth of an inch of motion made her eyes roll back and her nerve endings ring. There was no way to come on this rollercoaster of sensation. It was an experience more like an orgasm than any other part of sex, but it just kept on happening, peaking, cresting, climbing higher and peaking again" (Pat Califia, *Macho Sluts*).

These violent fluctuations of affect, these detours of wasted energy, leaving their traces on photographic plates, coursing incessantly through the bodies of Sherman's multiple personalities, also force their way into the viewer's tender and receptive flesh. I can't look at these pictures calmly. I feel myself falling, being sucked inexorably into them, losing my self-possession, gradually letting go. I become what I behold. Subject and object are now utterly indistinguishable, agitated or paralyzed by the same intense emotion. Isn't that what it means to be a woman? Why call it "castration," when it involves a heightening of sensory enjoyment? Doctor Schreber finds the loss of his "virility" a small price to pay for the increase in "voluptuousness" all over his body. And remember the plight of James Woods in Cronenberg's *Videodrome*. He becomes so passionate and deliriously passive a TV viewer that a vaginal slit opens up in his belly, a handy slot for inserting videocassettes directly. You macho asshole, now you know what it's like to be a cunt. Obtrusive men will ask the Freudian question, "what do women want?" But that's the sort of thing only cops and critics worry about. They'd never address such a question to themselves. It could only be directed at somebody else: somebody whose intimate touch they wish to avoid, but whose behavior they seek to control. And it's not a question we are willing or even able to answer, caught up as we are in the throes of desperation or abject rapture. Bodies pushed to such extremities no longer 'know' what they 'want.' "I can know what someone else is thinking, not what I am thinking," as Wittgenstein put it. Like the heroine of a Harlequin romance, or like a hot bitch in a porno flick, I'm absorbed and consumed by the intensities of the moment. There's no room here for a desire that would pause for self-reflection, or demand "recognition," or be predicated upon "lack." Everything implodes into this body, into this image, as into a black hole or a cunt. The feeling is orgasmic, but without that sense of culmination and finality that a 'real' orgasm provides. She might just as well be faking it, for all you know or understand. Men never fathom women's depths, Nietzsche says, not because women are "deep," but because they "aren't even shallow."

So forget your virile anxieties about whether you were able to make me come, about who I am and what I want, about what is authentically real and what is not. A woman's impetuous desire scorns such niceties of masculine logic. So what if I'm faking it? Do you suppose that your oh-so-precious manhood is any less of an imposture? You'd better wake up, babe. Everything is a simulacrum, everything is a cliché. Intuitions without thoughts are blind, or so they say; a passion that doesn't scruple to "know itself" is indistinguishable from an empty stereotype. You've seen it a million times before. I'm always playing a pre-given part, whether by cynical calculation, or because I've been swept up in the heat of the moment. Just like any woman, I'm not responsible for my actions. I'm literally beside myself. I lose myself when you make me come, but I equally lose myself when I act the virgin or the whore, when I flatter your male vanity by pretending that you are the only man for me or that you are able to make me come. "I is an other," remember, and that other is always a pre-programmed social or biological construction.

It's all theater, all feminine coquetry and affectation. Life is a long process of method acting. Try it, you'll like it. Just don't imagine that, beyond all the clichés, beneath all these particulars of sensation, affect, and personality, you will ever discover such a thing as 'yourself.' The obsessive serial repetitions and continual variations of Sherman's images should be enough to disabuse you of that notion. Which is why it's not enough just to "read" these photographs as "critiques," as didactic, illustrational depictions of oppressive gender roles; though plenty of critics have tried. Even Craig Owens, one of the best, argues that Sherman's images work "to expose the identification of the self with an image as its dispossession," and that they force upon the viewer "the urgent necessity of making a distinction" between actual women and the "alienating identifications" imposed upon them by the "false mirror" of mass media. But is that really the story here? The problem lies in Owens' recourse to the old modernist notion of "alienation." For in postmodern media space, there is no longer a *self* for one to be dispossessed of, or alienated from. Electronic media haven't alienated or perverted or destroyed human nature; rather, we must say that they *are* human nature. There is no virgin ground; the Outside is also populated by masks and stereotypes. Owens knows this well enough; he acknowledges Sherman's "complicity" with the very forces that perform the social construction and stereotyping of femininity. But the whole situation makes him uneasy. Doesn't such complicity threaten to undermine the very possibility of an oppositional stance? Well, not necessarily, once we reflect that it equally compromises the integrity of the forces of conformity and order themselves. Double agents are notorious for their unstable loyalties; they like to swing both ways. Yes, capitalism can co-opt anything; but co-optation too has its price. Owens tries to resolve the dilemma by invoking "the unavoidable necessity of participating in the very activity that is being denounced *precisely in order to denounce it.*" But isn't that making things a bit too easy? Let us not disavow the abject pleasures that complicity gives us, the urgency with which we are drawn to it, the strange desire that it inspires. It's time to discover the feminine delights of what Jean Genet calls *treason*.

I don't mean to deny the profoundly feminist import of Sherman's work, quite the contrary. I, too, yearn to become a woman. And woman is never the same. Her explosive proliferation in Sherman's "self-portraits" breaks the links of dependency, ruptures the chain of habit. But this is precisely why we can't confine Sherman's images to a critical awareness of the gender codes they travesty, or reduce them to the lessons and messages they seem to imply. It's not the meat, it's the motion. Politics begins in the ecstasy, suffering, and vulnerability of our agitated flesh. Sherman isn't content just to expose and critique social constructions of femininity; she gets off on the whole process far too much. She gleefully relishes—indeed, she prolongs and reiterates—the violent, intrusive movements of feminine fabrication. She takes a cruel, giddy delight in playing dress-up, in rummaging through heaps of old clothes, in twisting mannequin parts into grotesque new configurations. Bloody menstrual wounds, beautiful flowers of passion. Sherman floods the market with monstrous feminine simulacra. Each new self-portrait is yet another stylization of fetishized femininity, one more prosthetic proxy for an unpresentable self. These stereotypes are inscribed and effaced, again and again, one after another: constructed and deconstructed, affirmed and forgotten, in the same delirious motion.

The violent intensities of Sherman's photographs are thus a product of the most blatant artifice. These pictures obey the first rule of feminine imposture: just flaunt it shamelessly enough, and everybody will think you've really got it. Femininity is masquerade, as the psychoanalysts put it. Like a low-budget horror film, Sherman's work revels in its tongue-in-cheek sensationalism, its ostentatious phoniness, its use of gross and sleazy special effects. Take the images of food and debris from a 1987 series: puke spewed over an abandoned banquet; fat, repulsive worms swimming in snot sauce and heaped on a plate; decaying body parts immersed in beds of gravel and quicksand, lit to a lurid pink or blue. These images may be ludicrously cheesy, but they manage to disturb you all the same. Your own viscera are extracted, and served up to you on a platter. Death and decay are presented for your delectation, just like tits and ass on the Playboy Channel. No alienation-effect at work here; your excitement and revulsion are only heightened when you realize that you've been cheated, that none of this is really happening, that it's all only a spectacle mounted for your benefit. It's just like phone sex and peep shows. The nauseous intimacy of Sherman's sex dolls is all the more obscene for being forced and contrived, instead of spontaneous and open. Anyone with a little experience of s&m knows that the hokiest scenarios are the most effective at pushing bodies over the edge and into an uncontrollable frenzy. You've been a bad girl. Daddy wants to fuck. Mommy's gonna punish you. Lie still and let Nurse give you an enema.

It's all calculated and programmed, it's all just a performance. Yet everything screams vulnerability and pain. Don't even bother to ask whether woman is a product of nature or of culture. Femininity is a mutable construct, not an unchanging essence, regardless of whether chromosomes or social norms do the constructing. Sociobiologists may well be right when they claim that certain gender traits are written in our genes. Is that a problem? Given current levels of technology, it's far easier to rewrite or override the instructions of DNA than it would be to alter the harsh imperatives of the so-called Symbolic order. Sherman's prosthetic reconstructions of the flesh suggest that anatomy may in fact be our best hope for escaping the "destiny" of gender. As far as feminism is concerned, genetic engineering, hormone treatments, and plastic surgery are all better bets than psychoanalysis. Who needs a cock anyway? "It is man whom we must now make up our minds to emasculate ... Man is sick because he is badly constructed" (Artaud). So welcome to Dr. Sherman's operating table. Open up to me. Relax your sphincters.

Let the images penetrate your flesh, and burn into your retinas. Make their vulnerability your own. How do you think it feels? This isn't a critique; this is a slide into the depths of abjection. Everything enters through a gash, a slit, an open sore: the mouth, the eyes, the asshole, the cunt. Think of how Bataille describes Madame Edwarda's cunt, the divine shrine at which he ecstatically worships: "a live wound, gaping at me, hairy and pink, bursting with life like a repulsive octopus." Now, there's no turning back. This is not "lack," but overfullness, life lived to its greatest intensity.

8.

KATHY

ACKER

What was it you whispered to me, that last night we were together? "The communication joining lovers depends on the nakedness of their laceration. Their love signifies that neither can see the being of the other but only a wound and a need to be ruined. No greater desire exists than a wounded person's need for another wound." Your voice was tender, but matter-of-fact, without a trace of urgency. I didn't understand that this was your way of saying good-bye. Only later did I realize that you had been quoting Bataille. And so we bled into each other, slowly, in the dark. At daybreak you left. I never saw you again. I needed your wound, but since that night you've withheld it from me. Instead, you've hurt me far more with your absence. Now my lust, my longing, can never be assuaged. "I wish I could eat your cancer," as Kurt Cobain sang.

Why is it, Deleuze asks, that every love, every experience, every *event*, scars and shatters us? "Why is every event a kind of plague, war, wound, or death?" We are never equal to the event, Deleuze says, but always too early or too late, too frenzied or too passive, too forward or too withdrawn. Either it is "my life which seems too weak for me, and slips away"; or else "it is I who am too weak for life, it is life which overwhelms me, scattering its singularities all about, in no relation to me." Either way, my love for you is a lost opportunity, a missed encounter. The events that move me, that affect me, that relate me to you, are precisely the ones that I am unable to grasp. It isn't me and it isn't you, Bataille says, but *something else* that passes between us: "*what goes from one person to another* when we laugh or make love." Something lost in the instant, over as soon as it happens. Something inhuman, at the limits of communication. "Life doesn't exist inside language: too bad for me" (this is Kathy Acker, in *My Mother: Demonology*, appropriating, translating, and rewriting—channelling, in short— the voice of Colette Peignot, better known as Laure, Bataille's lover). I can't hold on to your life, or your love; I can only retain the trace of its passage, in the form of a scar. That's why every communication involves laceration. You got through to me only when you left a mark on my skin: a bruise, a puncture, a gash, an amputation, a burn. I was never able to possess the softness of your touch, the roughness with which you fucked me, the mocking irony of your voice. They were all too much for me, and vanished into the night. Only the memories remain, grotesque memorials etched ruinously into my flesh. Every line, every scar, concretizes your absence. For we suffer from reminiscences, and every reminiscence is a wound: whether slashed across the epidermis, or hacked out by the fraying of neural pathways in the brain.

It's difficult to realize just how sensitive skin really is. Even the slightest breath sets it all aquiver. Even the oldest slash or bite never entirely disappears. The skin, like any membrane, serves two complementary functions. Functions that are both so vitally necessary that "no life without a membrane of some kind is known" (Lynn Margulis and Dorion Sagan). On one hand, the skin marks a boundary, separates the inside from the outside. It guarantees the distinction between me and the world. It protects me from the insatiability of your desire; it preserves my guts from spilling out, and oozing in a sticky, shapeless mass all over the floor. But on the other hand, the skin (like any membrane) is not an absolute barrier; its pores, orifices and chemical gradients facilitate all sorts of passages and transfers. All along this surface, inside and outside come into intimate contact. Nutrients are absorbed, poisons excreted, signals exchanged. This is how I remember you, flesh sliding over flesh. My skin is the limit that confines me to myself; but it's also the means by which I reach out to you. It's like the prison walls Blanchot writes about, that both isolate the inmates one from another, and allow them to communicate by tapping and banging. What would happen if these walls were to come tumbling down? Could either of us endure a nakedness so extreme? How could we talk, how could we see, how could we touch one another? The exquisite pain of nerve endings in immediate contact . . . "Making love is such an entire negation of isolated existence," Bataille enthuses, "that we find it natural, even wonderful in a sense, that an insect dies in the consummation it sought out." But I didn't die when you came to me and when you fucked me; alas, I didn't even die when you left me. "I wanted us to be so naked with each other," Acker/Laure writes to Bataille, "that the violence of my passion was amputating me for you." But "as soon as you saw that I got pleasure from yielding to you, you turned away from me . . . You stated that you were denying me because you needed to be private. But what's real to you isn't real to me. I'm not you. Precisely: my truth is that for me your presence in my life is absence."

Which is why there is always a wound, whether of penetration or abandonment. We know that there can be no final nakedness. No last ecstatic unveiling of desire. Flay my skin, and all you'll do is uncover another layer. Fuck me hard, again and again, but it's never hard enough. "Love makes this demand," Bataille himself warned me: "either its object escapes you or you escape it. If love didn't run away from you, you'd run away from love." That's how I measured your distance from me, even before you left me. Your sweat, your saliva, your odors, your secretions: they penetrated every last one of my orifices and pores. But that's precisely how I knew that it was you. You seeped into my body like a beautiful toxin. Your alien stench remained, never losing itself in mine. The more our flesh intermingled, the more aware I became of your difference, your indifference, your utter separation. I spent hours tracing your piercings and tattoos, unreadable signs, like the armor and display of an alien species. But isn't this torment really what I sought from you? It was your strangeness, your haughty coldness— your irony, in short—that so captivated me. Who knows what cruelties and deceptions you nurtured just for me, even from the very first time we met? Who knows with what subtle poisons you nourished my blood? "As soon as I see that I need you," Acker/ Laure tells Bataille, "I imagine your absence. Again and again I'm picturing you rejecting me. This is the moment I love." I felt you most powerfully at the moment of your departure. The proof that you were real (and not just my fantasy) is that, when the time came, *you simply weren't there for me*. I secretly always knew that you would escape me in the end, and so I tried to make your betrayal mine.

And that, I think, was my deepest reason for going under the needle. "Getting pierced and tattooed tends to develop a person's awareness of *memory*," says the great tattoo artist Vyvyn Lazonga; tattoos "can function as physical reminders of something very meaningful that happened in the past, and stand alone as a powerful statement of who the person is or is becoming." These inscriptions in our living flesh are markers of intensity, memorials to impermanence and change. I resolved to monumentalize what I couldn't forget in any case. I cherished these wounds, for they were all that you left me. Rather than mourning your absence, I emblazoned it in all its glory. Each stab of the needle renewed the tang of another memory, polished another facet of my joy and humiliation. "There was pain; the pain was sharp and particular; the pain was so particular that he was able to isolate it . . . Dreams are made actual through pain" (Acker). A figure slowly emerged, my totem animal, a spider in black and red. Carapace, poison sac, eight articulated legs, crawling flush with my shoulder. Pain, rather than death, is the mother of beauty. I didn't abjure my suffering; I transformed it into adornment. I made myself into a work of art, as Wilde and Foucault recommend. Look at me now. These tracings aren't on my skin, they are my skin. Postmodern art of surfaces, pulsations of the membrane. "A strafing of the surface," Deleuze calls it, "in order to transmute the stabbing of bodies." It's impossible to distinguish now between literal and metaphorical levels of meaning, between sensuous images and intellectual symbols, or between physical and metaphysical wounds. They all flow together in the folds and ripples of my flesh. "My wound existed before me, I was born to embody it" (Joe Bousquet).

And there lies the whole problem of communication, does it not? What goes in, what comes out, what gets transmitted across the membrane? I thought I was self-sufficient, but desire made me porous. Every symbolic articulation, every inscription of meaning, leaves a scar on my flesh. Every particle of sense is a kind of contamination, an antigen coursing through my bloodstream. That's why dialogue is impossible. For me, it's only my wounds and piercings that can talk. Now that you've left me, you tell me that of course we'll always be friends; but I'm not sure I want that sort of friendship. Hello, how are you, I'm fine, have a nice day: is this what it all comes down to? Interchangeable selves in a perfectly uniform world, so that one fuck, one lover, is just as good as another? That's your ideal of transparent communication: everything already agreed to in advance, so there's no danger of misunderstanding or conflict. I would have nothing to tell you in such a world, and you would mean nothing special to me. How convenient for you! It's precisely for this that Acker/Laure reproaches Bataille: "You believe that everything that's outside you ('reality') is a reflection of your perceptions, thoughts, ideas, etc. In other words, that you can see, feel, hear, understand the world. Other people." You think that all our problems could easily be resolved, if only we would sit around and talk them through calmly. Well, maybe friends converse that way, but surely lovers do not. And you claim to have a self that's coherent with the rest of the world. But not me; I certainly don't. "I don't believe that," Acker/Laure goes on, "I believe that I'm so apart from the world, from other people, that I have to explain everything to every single person to such an extent in order to communicate at all that, for

me, communication's almost impossible." The moment you
wanted and wounded me, you wrenched me apart from the
world—and what's more, even worse, from myself. That very
instant, I ceased to be a coherent, communicating self. My being
was splayed, instead, upon the cross of your disregard. "I'm not an
enclosed or self-sufficient being" (Acker/Laure) any longer. There's
no common measure between the "I" and the "you."

And that's why pleasure alone just isn't enough. "We're alive
only at the top of the crest," says Bataille, "a flag flying high as the
ship goes down. With the slightest relaxation, the banality of
pleasure or boredom would supervene." Most Americans hate
pleasure, especially someone else's: hence the moralizing
campaigns today against smoking and drugs and promiscuity and
obscenity. But Bataille's objection is altogether different. He's
concerned rather with the feebleness, the mundanity of our
pleasures. A pleasure that truly affirmed itself would turn into
something else. "Any sensation," no matter how pleasurable, as
Pat Califia says, "that continues without a pause will eventually
be perceived as painful, especially if it increases in intensity."
And "many of us," she adds, "do court pain and welcome it.
There's the burn that runners pant for, the ache an athlete in
training prizes. Pain is also a signal that an emotional impasse (an
old conflict, buried grief) is being released. Pain can be a signal that
sensation is returning to a part of the body or psyche that has
gone numb." I can't separate the past from the present, I can't
help myself; I scratch at these scars until they bleed afresh. Isn't
that the difference between "me" and "you"? For you, pleasure is
a kind of stasis that pacifies the self: "a way of interrupting
desire, of instantly discharging it, and unburdening oneself of it"
(Deleuze and Guattari). You're like Freud, who sees pleasure as a
rehearsal for easeful death, the reduction of stress and excitation
to zero. But what good is that to me, who no longer have a self?
It's only pain that proves that I still exist. I can't discharge my
desire, I can't lull it to sleep. I need you so much, you can
never give me enough, you can never make me come. "In want,"
Acker/Laure cries, "everything is always being risked; being

is being overturned and ends up on the other side."

So: imagine a skin, a membrane, that's been inverted, twisted inside out. The immense universe of otherness is now compressed within its fragile walls. While the entrails extend beyond it, stretching outward to infinity. That's what my life has been like, since I encountered you. The otherness within me is more than I can bear. My being is dispersed, beyond what I can reach. I've gone so far already; how much further can I go? "Me, I'm insufficient, all I am is fantasies that tear 'me' apart . . . My life's disintegrating under me, whatever is 'I' are the remnants" (Acker/Laure). You slay me when you touch me, and even more when you ignore me; I get so hot and excited that I can't imagine any respite. Each encounter with you is a kind of death; but I'll never have done with dying. That first night, you tied me up, and left me alone in the dark. I don't know how long I was suspended there, waiting for your return. It was "a time without negation, without decision . . . without end, without beginning . . . without a future" (Blanchot). I hung like a fly in a spider's web, a naked singularity. That's when I altogether lost control, when your existence reached out and usurped the place of mine. All my inhibitions crumbled; there was room only for your absence. I realized that "the opposite of love is indifference, not hate" (Kathe Koja), and that the only true opposite of fantasy is pain. You were real, just like an itch that one is unable to scratch. If you didn't come back to release me, well, that was only to be expected: for there are never enough sadists for the masochists we mostly are. But I comforted myself by recalling Laurie Weeks' Theory of Total Humiliation: "we don't erect monolithic reified barriers **against** the humiliation; rather we welcome it, embrace it; then everyone wants to fuck us, for mysterious reasons."

It was only then that I understood Bataille's terrible irony. I realized that his well-advertised anguish was something of a ruse, and that beneath it lay an incredible distance and coldness. "The time has come to be hard. I have no option but to turn into stone . . . Is the pursuit of pleasure something cowardly? Yes, it seeks satisfaction. Desire, on the other hand, is avid not to be satisfied." It's not a matter, then, of frustration or of "lack," but of dissatisfaction deliberately sought out. I don't simply find myself in this state of agony; I've got to actively provoke it. I drink, not to be drunk, but to induce the next day's hangover. When you fuck me, I try not to come, but to hold off as long as possible. There's always something slightly phony about Bataille's porno fiction, when he revels in impiety and blasphemy, or when he tells us that nudity is obscene. Sure, let the priest drink his own piss from the communion cup. Sure, let Pierre be scandalized by his mother's bisexual debauchery. Sure, let Madame Edwarda run naked through the streets of Paris, like a savage beast. But what makes these stories so sexy and disturbing isn't that, or isn't that alone. It's more the sense we get that all these transgressions have somehow been staged; that the guilt and dread have been *assumed* by Bataille, for the sake of emotional effect. It's roleplaying, or performance, very much in the spirit of s&m. Isn't this what makes Bataille seem so, well, postmodern? Only by means of such corny fictions can we put ourselves at risk. Only through such exquisite irony can we shatter our everyday bourgeois selves, and accede to the heights of intense, impersonal passion. It's a bit like children playing with matches, after watching *Beavis and Butt-head*. For Bataille, there's not much difference between the heedlessness of a child, and the cynical apathy of the Marquis de Sade's heroes. Neither the child nor the jaded libertine believes that e has a self. Neither reposes for long in the stasis of satisfaction. Neither accepts responsibility for eir actions. It's all a matter of ignoring limits, and pushing things just a little bit too far . . . Bataille records that a certain Wartberg, with whom Laure lived in Berlin, "had her wear dog collars, put her on a leash, made her walk four-legged, and beat her with a stick." Bow-wow. Isn't that much like the story of how you treated me? But whatever you made me do, oh yes I wanted it. And however much you neglected and abandoned me, oh yes, I reveled in it. You drove me to the brink of ruin, indeed you did; but don't presume to think that that makes you the winner. My loss of control, my hysteria, was more than a match for your niggardly airs of detachment.

"How long does it take a man," William Burroughs asks, "to learn that he does not, cannot want what he 'wants'?" I only learn it, he suggests, when I have "reached the end of words, the end of what can be done with words." Bataille, too, insists that "the world of words is laughable. Threats, violence, and the blandishments of power are part of *silence*. Deep complicity can't be expressed in words... I'm only silence, and the universe is silence." Communication is unthinkable, literally unspeakable; only our wounds wordlessly touch one another. My mouth won't speak; like my other orifices, it's just a gaping sore. "I'm so horny when I awake," Acker/Laure writes to Bataille, "I place my fingers in your mouth so you can bite them, only the mouth I'm placing them in is my own." In this silence, this separation, my identity disappeared; only this body remained, this pierced and wounded skin. I don't know what I want any more, perhaps it isn't even you. I could have told you what Marguerite Duras told Bataille one day: "you lived this love in the only manner possible for you, by losing it before it arrived." But I didn't say it; for what use are words and more words? After you left me, I didn't know where to turn. Intense, impersonal moods swept over me, coming and going in waves; I thought I was going to break, and I half hoped that I would. I wanted to kill those parts of me that loved and hated you; I wanted to escape them, I wanted to kill myself. But I found that I couldn't: the endlessness of my longing always returned. "I tried everything," Acker/Laure says, "to lose myself, to get rid of memory, to resemble whom I don't resemble, to end... I tried to give my life away and life came back, gushed into its sources, the stream, the storm, into the full of noon, *triumphant*, and it stayed there hidden, like a lightning stain."

9. DANIEL PAUL SCHREBER

It's all happening in the depths of my body, in the twists of my bowels, in the leaps across my synapses, in the nucleic acid transfers of my cells. So much activity, not even ceasing when I try to sleep. Doctor Daniel Paul Schreber discovers that he is being turned into a woman, as *nerves of voluptuousness* grow throughout his body; these nerves are constantly being stimulated to a pitch of orgasmic excitement. He must perpetually listen to the voices of dead souls and innumerable little birds, speaking to him in the *nerve-language*, "an empty babble of ever recurring monotonous phrases in tiresome repetition." He complains of the *compulsive thinking* that he is forced to endure, a process of "having to think continually," in opposition to "man's natural right of mental relaxation, of temporary rest from mental activity through thinking nothing." Never a moment in which not to think and feel. Machines within me, engines in hyperdrive, factories in constant overproduction. Bataille argues that nature and capitalism alike are driven not by scarcity, but by excess, a superabundance that we are unable to discharge: "The sun dispenses energy—wealth—without any return. The sun gives without ever receiving." My own body is suffused with such surplus. But it is impossible to emulate the sun, impossible for me ever to spend or squander enough. No wonder I find it difficult to get enough sleep. Schreber, suffering under the weight of this irreversible generosity, unable to suspend his exquisite *soul-voluptuousness* and pay off his debt, screams that the sun is a whore, and identifies it with God.

Even when the sun is gone, its excessive, radiant energy still refuses to subside. Afterimages assault me. Or else the night has its own agitations and terrors, like those encountered by Blanchot's Thomas the Obscure: "It was night itself. Images which constituted its darkness inundated him." Schreber is dazzled by nocturnal, no less than diurnal, radiance. The onset of his nervous illness is signaled when malign forces conspire to deprive him of rest: "a recurrent cracking noise in the wall of our bedroom became noticeable at shorter or longer intervals; time and again it woke me as I was about to go to sleep." Like Poe's and Lovecraft's narrators, I am unable to exorcise the merest hint of sound, a vibration just beneath the threshold of clear and distinct perception. Insomnia is the bane of my existence. It keeps me awake and alert just enough so that I cannot enjoy the refreshment of rest; but not sufficiently so for me to be able to compose and collect my thoughts. And so I find myself staring into the semidarkness, endlessly repeating fragments from unfinished dreams. Emmanuel Levinas thus describes insomnia as a state of anonymous, impersonal *vigilance*. My thoughts are tiresomely meticulous, my attention is painstakingly thorough; but I can't lay hold of anything concrete. The sense of a centered, stable selfhood dissolves; all this thought and attention belongs to nobody and is "suspended on *nothing*." There is no hope of bringing anything to a conclusion: I have to follow the very same steps, answer the same objections, count the same sheep, over and over again. "I'll never know, in the silence you don't know, you must go on, I can't go on, I'll go on" (Beckett). It's not fear of death or deprivation that haunts me; rather it's the very exuberance of existence, this *having always to go on*, that becomes an ironic burden. If only I could sleep.

When will it all stop, we ask, how much longer can we stand it? "From a certain point of view it would be much better if nothing worked, if nothing functioned. Never being born, escaping the wheel of continual birth and rebirth, no mouth to suck with, no anus to shit through" (Deleuze and Guattari). Postmodern culture is pervaded by such apocalyptic imaginings, fears and longings. We are peculiarly obsessed with *doom*, with the end of the world. **DOOM PATROL**, living up to its name, is filled with signs and portents of the Last Things, barely averted threats of universal destruction. Our dread is only the flip side of a restless fascination, a deep yearning that arises in long nights of insomniac vigilance. Sometimes we want everything to stop, to die, just so that we can sink into final oblivion, together with all the rest. The pleasure of making the world come to an end is much like the pleasure of finally being able to take a shit. For Schreber, "liberation from the pressure of faeces present in the guts creates an intense feeling of well-being, particularly for the nerves of voluptuousness." But God, who is ignorant of how living beings actually feel, who only really understands sleepers and corpses, translates this sense of well-being into the delusion that shitting equals death, that taking a shit "is to a certain extent the final act" for any living organism. God wants both to push Schreber to the point of death, in order to withdraw from his excessive attraction, and to maintain Schreber alive in a state of unresolved voluptuousness, in order thereby to expropriate that voluptuousness for his own sustenance. And so, trapped in this ambivalent double bind, God tortures Schreber by producing in him the imperious urge to shit, while simultaneously denying him the ability to do so.

The logic of insomnia, like that of constipation, moves in a vicious circle of evasion and control. I agitate myself all the more, the more I strive to relax and establish peace. Whenever I seek release, I find myself invoking the very "miraculous" forces from which I am also trying to escape. Life's "extreme exuberance," Bataille writes, "pours out in a movement always bordering on explosion": an explosion that is always impending, but that never actually arrives. The compulsive thoughts and movements that deny me rest are the same ones that threaten to devastate the world; and so I only increase my own torment when I call upon them to unleash an ultimate catastrophe. Schreber finds that the divine rays that invest his own body with unbearably heightened sensation have also annihilated the earth, the heavens, and the entire rest of mankind. He is constrained within Being, made to live through his own destruction, to feel the evisceration of his organs, to endure more than any living organism possibly could endure. The apocalyptic vision of universal ruin is in this way itself the nightmare that interrupts my sleep, and throws me back upon the torments of involuntary wakefulness. And so I toss and turn in my bed, trying out every posture except the right one, the unique one in which my body would finally be able to relax.

These divine or infernal machines are at work in our bodies, and all throughout society. It seems that they are on the verge of destroying everything, but it also seems that they will remain forever in motion, insuring for all eternity that there is something rather than nothing. Schreber eventually realizes that the old world, which has palpably collapsed all around him, nonetheless continues to function in its accustomed manner. The process of his *unmanning* is inexorable, but it will take millennia. Quite similarly, the bewildered heroes of **DOOM PATROL** find themselves trying to combat strange apocalyptic forces that on one level menace the existence of the world absolutely, yet on another level seem to leave everything intact. In one series of episodes, a Gnostic sect called the Cult of the Unwritten Book summons the Decreator, God's dark double, who will reverse the order of the creation of the universe and return everything to the nothingness whence it came. The process of decreation is unstoppable and irreversible, much like entropy; but our heroes are able to slow it down, so that it will take billions of years to accomplish itself—the same length of time as for the entropic heat-death of the universe—instead of just a couple of days. The Apocalypse is in effect, but its progress is so slackened as to be nearly imperceptible.

In another series of episodes, a *psychic apocalypse* is visible only to "children, lunatics, and sensitives"; the spectacle of "New York ablaze, overrun by screaming phantoms" simply isn't noticed by anybody else. The Apocalypse, in this version, may be called *virtual* (as when we speak of 'virtual images') rather than *actual*, since it affects not the immediate experiential world but "the soul of the world, the world's dream of itself." But such a virtual event is perfectly real, as Deleuze repeatedly says, even if it isn't actual; the psychic apocalypse, like a neutron bomb, may leave physical structures untouched, but it turns human society into a collection of "dead shells, zombie cultures, shambling aimlessly towards oblivion." In wiping out the world's dreams, it reduces us to a state of insomniac unfulfillment: we are dead in effect, but we are compelled like zombies to live through and testify again and again to our death. The agent responsible for this virtual destruction is called the Candlemaker: it has emerged from the virtual, traumatically charged realm of nursery rhymes and childhood imaginings. Dorothy Spinner, the teenaged girl who is the newest member of the **DOOM PATROL**, has the ability to project her innermost imaginings onto the plane of consensus reality; but she is more the victim than the master of this power. Her brain is overloaded with scary childhood memories, and anxieties over her first menstruation. Fantasy, for her, implies bodily shock and trauma; childhood is forever charged with danger and loss. And so she imagines the Candlemaker into existence: "It makes candles for the dead, that's what it does; it has to kill everyone so it can make candles for them." It has to murder, that is, in order then to memorialize. Dorothy's mind is trapped in a horrific feedback loop. In the Candlemaker's virtual apocalypse, as in the delirium of Schreber and in the busy vacuousness of insomnia, the very drama of extinction prevents us from ever attaining nothingness.

In this sense, *postmodern* also means *postapocalyptic*. The modernists proclaimed the millennium, finalities and absolutes of all sorts. They projected triumphant aesthetic utopias, and they encountered equally unmitigated political horrors. History, they thought, was coming to its dialectically preordained conclusion; whether this end was blissful or horrible—socialism or fascism, technological paradise or nuclear holocaust—was only a secondary matter. But today, as the literal millennium approaches, we are more likely to conceive the end of life as we know it as an everyday and almost casual process, without a "final conflict" or an impressive, stirring narrative climax. All through the Cold War we were waiting for an ultimate cataclysm, some all-consuming event. But now that the Cold War is over, we have come to realize that nothing is ever *really* over. There are more wars and insecurities than ever before. It has been said that the only thing we learn from history is that we do not learn from history. Well, now we must confront the fact that the only "end of history" is that history is always ending, so that in fact there is no end to history. We're beginning to understand that there can be no release and no respite, not even in our dreams of destruction and renovation. "A screaming comes across the sky. It has happened before . . ." (Pynchon). It's all just business as usual: today is the first day of the rest of your life. Which is why our culture's privileged model of extinction is no longer nuclear war, but rather the excruciatingly slow, always-already-in-process, devastation of the environment. Ecological disaster is like constipation: nothing sudden, but a continuing inability to evacuate, expenditure blocked and turned against itself, a long-drawn-out and inconclusive torment, the slow poisoning of the bowels. Finality just won't come to an end. Nietzsche's most striking insight is not the banal modernist one that "God is dead," but the postmodernist qualification that "this tremendous deed is still on its way, still wandering . . . this deed is still more distant from [men] than the most distant stars—*and yet they have done it themselves*." We are still helplessly entangled in the endless ramifications and reverberations of modernism's supposed ultimates, as they perpetuate themselves to infinity; and that's the reason for the *post-* in postmodernism.

And so, we may say that the Apocalypse has already happened; or better, that it is happening right now, continually and inconclusively, even as we speak. Only nobody noticed. "Armageddon has been in effect; go get a late pass" (Public Enemy). Like the heroes of **DOOM PATROL**, we unwittingly find ourselves in the midst of the battle. *Doom* is no longer a distant horizon, a telos, an ultimate limit; it is all around us, it is the very air we breathe. We have already survived our own extinction, outlived the ends which alone gave our lives meaning. We already live on intimate terms with the forces that threaten to destroy us: they've simply become so ubiquitous that we take them for granted, and no longer pay them any special attention. The message, according to Jean Baudrillard, is "that the catastrophe is already there, that it has already occurred *because the very idea of the catastrophe is impossible.*" Schreber realizes that he has only further seduced and excited the divine rays by trying vigorously to resist them; and so he comes to welcome their efforts to penetrate and unman him. He simulates femininity, already becoming a woman in practice by decking his body with "feminine adornments" and devoting himself to "the cultivation of voluptuousness," even as he waits for the interminably delayed miracle that will definitively feminize him. The word *apocalypse* literally means *disclosure* or *revelation*, the prophetic uncovering of last things; but in common speech it has come to mean those last things themselves. This displacement is appropriate, since the postmodern world is precisely one in which whatever may be revealed of the future has in fact already unfolded in the present. "The boundary between science fiction and social reality is an optical illusion," says Donna Haraway. Our incessant waiting for catastrophe to happen itself enfolds or embodies the catastrophic event.

This is why so much of postmodern thought is concerned with events *after* the end of the world. Military think tanks generate contingency plans for "the day after" a massive thermonuclear exchange. I also recall a Trotskyist fringe group, the Posadaists, that preached the virtues of "revolutionary nuclear war." Such reckless calculations may scandalize many, but science fiction writers have long been doing the same. Philip K. Dick and J. G. Ballard both regard catastrophe not as the culmination of life, but as a precondition, and even a stimulus, for continued action. With disingenuous blitheness, Dick suggests that his *Dr. Bloodmoney* "is an extremely hopeful novel," because it "does not posit the end of human civilization as a result of the next war. People are still around and they are still coping." Indeed, they are "coping," in this and in other of Dick's postapocalyptic novels, with vast paranoid conspiracies, with crippling ontological doubts about the reality of everything they experience, and with mutants whose magical powers and manias for control lead them to inflict new forms of suffering; but this doesn't much change things. For Dick's point is that apocalyptic tremors, like psychedelic drugs, don't do anything other than force us to be more fully aware of the horrors (and the joys) that we are experiencing already. It would be superfluous to dread the onset of those very conditions (ubiquitous commodification, media manipulation, conspiratorial bureaucracies) that already shape our everyday life under late capitalism. We are compelled to acknowledge such forces, just as Descartes was compelled to posit the existence of God. If Ronald Reagan didn't exist, it would be necessary to invent him.

Many of Ballard's works are similarly set in the abandoned ruins of a superannuated industrial society, and depict a life that absurdly continues to flourish amidst rubble and ecological waste. Production has been abolished, and reproduced mass-media images circulate randomly and fragmentarily on their own, having outlived their ostensible purpose of creating demand and stimulating sales. In this postapocalyptic world, we are freed from what Reaganite and Thatcherite sado-monetarists like to call "the discipline of the market," but not for all that from the demands of nonproductive consumption and expenditure. Ballard fashions an affectless, yet strangely compelling, lyricism from our industrial and information-media leftovers. We are relegated to a life of restless scavenging for subsistence and for status; and we are beset by obsessive, futile dreams, now of orgasmic vehicular disasters, now of gliding in paradisiacal free flight and falling softly into the sun. "The optimum sex-death of Ronald Reagan" ("Why I Want to Fuck Ronald Reagan") on the one hand, and the beloved President's gentle, but inexorable, slide into senile dementia ("The Secret History of World War 3") on the other. For Reagan's miraculous body is our collective, postmodern equivalent of Doctor Schreber's: it suffers innumerable violent assaults and amputations, yet it remains untouched as a quasi-divine "substance of unity" (Kenneth Dean and Brian Massumi, *First and Last Emperors*). Ballard's obsessive catalogues of such things as radiation burns, wounds from auto accidents, spinal deformities, exploding helicopters, rusted machinery, ruined car parks, and fragments of enormous billboards, must be supplemented by those other strange and magical objects, the anal polyps and lacerating bullets and water on the brain, that surgeons are continually extracting from Reagan's flesh. The ex-President's glorious body, just like Schreber's, becomes increasingly saturated with voluptuousness: it evidences the messy afterbirths of a monstrous cataclysm that went unnoticed at the time, or that somehow never quite happened.

The postmodern Apocalypse is ubiquitous but invisible. The disaster never happens in the present, Blanchot says, for it is an abyss swallowing every presence and every present: "the disaster ruins everything while leaving everything in place." We cannot escape its overwhelming pressure, but we also cannot grasp it directly. It is happening now, but so subtly that we confuse it with everyday life; or else it has already happened, but so overwhelmingly as to have wiped out our memories of what things were like before. Let us then abandon the tired modernist rhetoric of crisis and loss. The superabundant energy that perturbs and threatens us, and that keeps us awake at night, will never be exhausted. Postmodern culture indeed displays a certain sense of urgency and impending doom, but one that is always being ironized, stylized, and indefinitely deferred. Even death, Bataille says, is a heightening of life, as it manifests life's irresistible propensity for the "luxurious squandering of energy in every form." Call it the Apocalypse if you like; but remember that the dinosaurs' destruction was our stroke of good fortune. The *limit* at which catastrophic expenditure occurs is not a finality; chaos theory tells us that it is rather a *singularity*, a point of *phase transition* or of metamorphosis. Niles Caulder, the Chief of the **DOOM PATROL**, reveals near the end of the series that he has deliberately, experimentally induced the calamitous events that transformed the members of the group into paranormal beings, discontented misfits with strange powers. Inspired by chaos theory, Caulder works to generate the "catastrophe curve," representing "the introduction of sudden, discontinuous change into a stable system. We cannot predict the effect of catastrophe, but we can use this model to help ascertain the conditions most favorable for its manifestation." Having produced catastrophe on an individual scale, he is now about to provoke it on a global scale, setting off a convulsion of such magnitude that all of humanity will "be forced to change and adapt." The Apocalypse thus appears not as a final consummation, but as a new Nietzschean throw of the dice, a fresh redistribution of "the movements of energy on the surface of the globe" (Bataille). Once we have started experimenting, we must go on to question everything: not to discover firm and unshakable foundations, but to make sure that nothing ever becomes that firm. Free from the conservative dread of disaster, and equally free from the nihilistic urge to bring everything to a final halt, Niles Caulder proclaims his "faith in the unexpected, the unpredictable . . . I believe in the catastrophe, I welcome it with open arms."

10. WILLIAM BURROUGHS

"Which came first, the intestine or the tapeworm?" In this epigram, Burroughs suggests that parasitism—corruption, plagiarism, surplus appropriation—is in fact conterminous with life itself. The tapeworm doesn't simply happen to attach itself to an intestine that was getting along perfectly well without it. Say rather that the intestine evolved in the way that it did just in order to provide the tapeworm with a comfortable or profitable milieu, an environment in which it might thrive. My intestines are on as intimate terms with their tapeworms as they are with my mouth, my asshole, and my other organs; the relationship is as 'intrinsic' and 'organic' in the one case as it is in the other. Just like the tapeworm, I live off the surplus-value extracted from what passes through my stomach and intestines. Who's the parasite, then, and who's the host? The internal organs are parasitic upon one another; the organism as a whole is parasitic upon the world. My 'innards' are really a hole going straight through my body; their contents—shit and tapeworm—remain forever outside of and apart from me, even as they exist at my very center. The tapeworm is more "me" than I am myself. My shit is my inner essence; yet I cannot assimilate it to myself, but find myself always compelled to give it away. (Hence Freud's equation of feces with money and gifts; and Artaud's sense of being robbed of his body and selfhood every time he took a shit). Interiority means intrusion and colonization. Self-identity is ultimately a symptom of parasitic invasion, the expression within me of forces originating from outside.

And so it is with language. In Burroughs' famous dictum, language is a virus. Language is to the brain (and the speaking mouth and the writing or typing hand, and the listening ear and the reading eyes) as the tapeworm is to the intestines. Even more so: it may just be possible to find a digestive space free from parasitic infection (though this is extremely unlikely), but we will never find an uncontaminated mental space. Strands of alien DNA unfurl themselves in our brains, just as tapeworms unfurl themselves in our guts. Burroughs suggests that not just language, but "the whole quality of human consciousness, as expressed in male and female, is basically a virus mechanism." This is not to claim, in the manner of De Saussure and certain foolish poststructuralists, that all thought is linguistic, or that social reality is constituted exclusively through language. It is rather to deprivilege language—and thus to take apart the customary opposition between language and immediate intuition—by pointing out that nonlinguistic modes of thought (which obviously exist) are themselves also constituted by parasitic infiltration. Visual apprehension and the internal time sense, to take just two examples, are both radically nonlinguistic; but they too, in their own ways, are theaters of power and surplus-value extraction. Light sears my eyeballs, leaves its traces violently incised on my retinas. Duration imposes its ungraspable rhythms, emptying me of my own thought. Viruses and parasitic worms are at work everywhere, multiple outsides colonizing our insides. There is no refuge of pure interiority, not even before language. Whoever we are, and wherever and however we search, "we are all tainted with viral origins."

Burroughs' formulation is of course deliberately paradoxical, since viruses are never originary beings. They aren't self-sufficient, or even fully alive; they always need to commandeer the cells of an already-existing host in order to reproduce. A virus is nothing but DNA or RNA encased in a protective sheath; that is to say, it is a message —encoded in nucleic acid—whose only content is an order to repeat itself. When a living cell is invaded by a virus, it is compelled to obey this order. Here the medium really is the message: for the virus doesn't enunciate any command, so much as the virus *is* itself the command. It is a machine for reproduction, but without any external or referential content to be reproduced. A virus is a simulacrum: a copy for which there is no original, emptily duplicating itself to infinity. It doesn't represent anything, and it doesn't have to refer back to any standard measure or first instance, because it already contains all the information—and only the information—needed for its own further replication. Marx's famous description of capital applies perfectly to viruses: "dead labor which, vampire-like, lives only by sucking living labor, and lives the more, the more labor it sucks."

Reproduction (sexual or otherwise) is often sentimentally regarded as the basic activity and fundamental characteristic of life. It's only through reproduction that natural selection does its work. But look a bit more closely: reproduction is arguably more a viral than a vital process. It is so far from being straightforwardly 'organic,' that it necessarily involves vampirism, parasitism, and cancerous simulation. We are all tainted with viral origins, because life itself is commanded and impelled by something alien to life. The life possessed by a cell, and all the more so by a multicellular organism, is finally only its ability to carry out the orders transmitted to it by DNA and RNA. It scarcely matters whether these orders originate from a virus, or from what we conceive as the cell's own nucleus. For this distinction is only a matter of practical convenience. It is impossible actually to isolate the organism in a state before it has been infiltrated by viruses, or altered by mutations; we cannot separate out the different segments of DNA, and determine which are intrinsic to the organism and which are foreign. Our cells' own DNA is perhaps best regarded as a viral intruder that has so successfully and over so long a stretch of time managed to insinuate itself within us, that we have forgotten its alien origin. Richard Dawkins suggests that our bodies and minds are merely "survival machines" for replicating genes, "gigantic lumbering robots" created for the sole purpose of transmitting DNA. Burroughs describes language (or sexuality, or any form of consciousness) as "the *human virus*." All our mechanisms of reproduction follow the viral logic according to which life produces death, and death in turn lives off life. And so remember this the next time you gush over a cute infant. "Cry of newborn baby gurgles into death rattle and the crystal skull," Burroughs writes, "THAT IS WHAT YOU GET FOR FUCKING."

Language is one of these mechanisms of reproduction. Its purpose is not to indicate or communicate any particular content, so much as to perpetuate and replicate itself. The problem with most versions of communications theory is that they ignore this function, and naively present language as a means of transmitting information. Yet language, like a virus or like capital, is in itself entirely vacuous: its supposed content is only a contingent means (the host cell or the particular commodity form) that it parasitically appropriates for the end of self-valorization and self-proliferation. Apart from the medium, there's no other message. But if language cannot be apprehended in terms of informational content, still less can it be understood on the basis of its form or structure, in the manner of Saussure, Chomsky, and their followers. Such theorists make an equivalent, but symmetrically opposite, error to that of communications theory. They substitute inner coherence for outer correspondence, differential articulation for communicative redundancy, self-reference for external reference; but by isolating language's self-relational structure or transformational logic, they continue to neglect the concrete and pragmatic effects of its violent replicating force. Both communicational and structural approaches try to define what language *is*, instead of looking at what it *does*. They both fail to come to grips with what J. L. Austin calls the *performative* aspect of linguistic utterance: the sense in which speaking and writing are *actions*, ways of doing something, and not merely ways of (con)stating or referring to something. (Of course, stating and referring are in the last analysis themselves actions). Language does not represent the world: it intervenes in the world, invades the world, appropriates the world. The supposed postmodern "disappearance of the referent" in fact testifies to the success of this invasion. It's not that language doesn't refer to anything real, but—to the contrary—that language itself has become increasingly real. Far from referring only to itself, language is powerfully intertwined with all the other aspects of contemporary social reality. It is a virus that has all too fully incorporated itself into the life of its hosts.

A virus has no morals, as Rosa von Praunheim puts it, talking about HIV; and similarly the language virus has no meanings. Even saying that language is performative doesn't go far enough; for it leaves aside the further question of what sort of act is being performed, and just *who* is performing it. It is not "I" who speaks, but the virus inside me. And this virus/speech is not a freestanding action, but a motivated and directed one: a command. Morse Peckham, Deleuze and Guattari, and Wittgenstein all suggest that language is less performative than it is imperative or prescriptive: to speak is to give orders. To understand language and speech is to acknowledge these orders: to obey them or resist them, but to react to them in some way. An alien force has taken hold of me, and I cannot *not* respond. Our bodies similarly respond with *symptoms* to infection, or to the orders of viral DNA and RNA. As Burroughs reminds us: "the symptoms of a virus are the attempts of the body to deal with the virus attack. By their symptoms you shall know them . . . if a virus produces no symptoms, then we have no way of knowing that it exists." And so with all linguistic utterances: I interpret a statement by reacting to it, which is to say by generating a symptom. Voices continually call and respond, invoke and provoke other voices. Speaking is thus in Foucault's sense an exercise of power: "it incites, it induces, it seduces, it makes easier or more difficult; in the extreme it constrains or forbids absolutely; it is nevertheless always a way of acting upon an acting subject or acting subjects by virtue of their acting or being capable of acting. A set of actions upon other actions." Usually we obey orders that have been given us, viscerally and unreflectively; but even if we self-consciously refuse them, we are still operating under their constraint, or according to their dictation. Yet since an order is itself an action, and the only response to an action is another action, what Wittgenstein ironically calls the "gulf between an order and its execution" always remains. I can reply to a performance only with another performance; it is impossible to step outside of the series of actions, to break the chain and isolate once and for all the 'true' meaning of an utterance. The material force of the utterance compels me to respond, but no hermeneutics can guarantee or legislate the precise nature of my response. The only workable way to define "meaning" is therefore to say, with Peckham, that it is radically arbitrary, since *any response to an utterance is a meaning of that utterance.*" Any response whatsoever. This accounts both for the fascistic, imperative nature of language, and for its infinite susceptibility to perversion and deviation. Strands of DNA replicate themselves *ad infinitum.* But in the course of these mindless repetitions, unexpected reactions spontaneously arise, alien viruses insinuate themselves into the DNA sequence, and radiation produces random mutations. It's much like what happens in the children's game 'Telephone': even when a sentence is repeated as exactly as possible, it tends to change radically over the course of time.

We all have parasites inhabiting our bodies; even as we are ourselves parasites feeding on larger structures. Call this a formula for demonic or vampiric possession. The great modernist project was to let the Being of Language shine forth, or some such grandiose notion. If "I" was not the speaker, the modernists believed, this was because language itself spoke to me and through me. Heidegger is well aware that language consists in giving orders, but he odiously idealizes the whole process of command and obedience. Today, we know better. We must say, contrary to Heidegger and Lacan, that language *never* "speaks itself as language": it's always some particular parasite, with its own interests and perspective, that's issuing the orders and collecting the profits. What distinguishes a virus or parasite is precisely that it has no proper relation to Being. It only inhabits somebody else's dwelling. Every discourse is an unwelcome guest that sponges off me, without paying its share of the rent. My body and home are always infested—whether by cockroaches and tapeworms, or by Martians and poltergeists. Language isn't the House of Being, but a fairground filled with hucksters and con artists. Think of Melville's Confidence Man; or Burroughs' innumerable petty operators, all pulling their scams. Michel Serres, in his book *The Parasite*, traces endless chains of appropriation and transfer, subtending all forms of communication. (He plays on the fact that in French the word *parasite* has the additional connotation of static, the noise on the line that interferes with or contaminates every message). In this incessant commerce, there is no Being of language. But there are always voices: voices and more voices, voices within and behind voices, voices interfering with, replacing, or capturing other voices.

I hear these voices whenever I speak, whenever I write, whenever I pick up the telephone. Marshall McLuhan argues that technological change literally produces alterations in the ratio of our senses. The media are artificially generated parasites, pros- thetic organs, "the extensions of man." Contemporary electronic media are particularly radical, as they don't just amplify one sense organ or another, but represent an exteriorization of the entire human nervous system. Today we don't need shamans any longer, since modems and FAXes are enough to put us in contact with the world of vampires and demons, the world of the dead. Viruses rise to the surface, and appear not just in the depths of our bodies, but visibly scrawled across our computer and video screens. In William Gibson's *Count Zero*, the Haitian loas manifest themselves in cyberspace: spirits arising in the interstices of our collectively extended neurons, and demanding propitiation. In **DOOM PATROL**, we learn that the telephone is "a medium through which ghosts might communicate"; words spoken over the phone are "a conjuration, a summoning." The dead are unable fully to depart from the electronic world. They leave their voices behind, resonating emptily after them. The buzzing or static that we hear on the telephone line is the sum of all the faint murmurings of the dead, blank voices of missed connections, echoing to infinity. These senseless utterances at once feed upon, and serve as the pre-conditions for, my own attempts to generate discourse. But such parasitic voices also easily become fodder for centralizing apparatuses of power, like the military's C³I system (command/control/communication/intelligence). **DOOM PATROL** reveals that the Pentagon is really a pentagram, "a spirit trap, a lens to focus energy." The "astral husks" of the dead are trapped in its depths, fed to the voracious Telephone Avatar, and put to work on the Ant Farm, "a machinery whose only purpose is to be its own sweet self." As Burroughs similarly notes, the life-in-death of endless viral replication is at once the method and the aim of postmodern arrangements of power.

No moribund humanist ideologies will release us from this dilemma. Precisely by virtue of their obsolescence, calls to subjective agency, or to collective imagination and mobilization, merely reinforce the feedback loops of normalizing power. For it is precisely by regulating and punishing ourselves, internalizing the social functions of policing and control, that we arrive at the strange notion that we are producing our own proper language, speaking for ourselves. Burroughs instead proposes a stranger, more radical strategy: "As you know inoculation is the weapon of choice against virus and inoculation can only be effected through exposure." For all good remedies are homeopathic. We need to perfect our own habits of parasitism, and ever more busily frequent the habitations of our dead, in the knowledge that every self-perpetuating and self-extending system ultimately encounters its own limits, its own parasites. Let us become dandies of garbage, and cultivate our own tapeworms, like Uncle Alexander in Michel Tournier's novel *Gemini* (*Les Météores*). Let us stylize, enhance, and accelerate the processes of viral replication: for thereby we increase the probability of mutation. In Burroughs' vision, "the virus plagues empty whole continents. At the same time new species arise with the same rapidity since the temporal limits on growth have been removed . . . The biologic bank is open." It's now time to spend freely, to mortgage ourselves beyond our means.

Don't try to express "yourself", then; learn rather to write from dictation, and to speak rapturously in tongues. An author is not a sublime creator, as Dr. Frankenstein wanted to be. E is more what is called a channeller, or what Jack Spicer describes as a radio picking up messages from Mars, or what Jacques Derrida refers to as a sphincter. Everything in Burroughs' fiction is resolved into and out of a spinning asshole, which is also finally a cosmic black hole. In Chester Brown's graphic novel *Ed the Happy Clown* (originally published in his comic book *Yummy Fur*), there is a man who suffers from a bizarre compulsion: he can't stop shitting. More comes out than he could ever possibly have put in. It turns out that his asshole is a gateway to another dimension, a transfer point between worlds. This other dimension isn't much different from ours: it has its own hierarchies of money and power, its own ecological dilemmas, and even its own Ronald Reagan. The interference between the two worlds leads to a series of hysterical sexual fantasies, grotesque amputations, and surreal confusions of identity. But what's important is the process of transmission, not the nature of the product. That's the secret of scatology: waste is the only wealth. "Why linger over books to which the author has not been palpably *constrained*?" (Bataille). This constraint, this pressure in my intestines and bowels, marks the approach of the radically Other. It's in such terms, perhaps, that we can best respond to George Clinton's famous exhortation: "Free your mind, and your ass will follow."

11. DAVID CRONENBERG

We all have our totem animals, our familiars, our spirit guides. They are usually other mammals, sometimes birds, occasionally even reptiles or amphibians; but they are almost always vertebrates of one sort or another. Our relationships with insects, on the other hand, tend to be stranger, more uncanny, more disturbing. Few of us—Spiderman aside—willingly accept intimacy with the arthropods. "Insect collecting is a hobby few can share," as Shonen Knife gently laments. Burroughs waxes lyrical about cats, about lemurs, about "sables, raccoons, minks, otters, skunks and sand foxes"; but he can only approach centipedes and insects with an obsessive, fascinated repulsion. Exceptions can perhaps be made for the beauty of butterflies, and the savoriness of certain non-insect arthropods, like crustaceans. But almost none of us enjoys our enforced proximity to bedbugs, cockroaches, and houseflies. Is our disgust simply the result of being confronted with a life form so utterly alien? Our lineage separated from theirs more than 600 million years ago, even before the Cambrian explosion. The insects' modes of feeding and fucking, those two most crucial biological functions, are irretrievably different from ours. Looking across the vast evolutionary gap, we are seized by vertiginous shudders of gastronomical nausea and sexual hysteria: "We have all seen nature films in which enormously magnified insects un-feelingly dismember their prey. Their glittering multifaceted eyes stare at the camera while their complex mouthparts work busily, munching through still-struggling victims. We can empathize with our closer relatives the lions, who at least seem to enjoy their bloody work. But when the female mantis bites the head off its mate in order to release its copulatory reflex, it does so at the behest of an instinct that seems to have nothing to do with love, hate, or anything else to which we can remotely relate" (Christopher Wills).

Such an enthralled disgust is crucial to the postmodern experience of limits. The narrator of Clarice Lispector's *The Passion According to G. H.* is captivated by the sight of a wounded cockroach, trapped in a doorjamb as a "whitish and thick and slow" paste oozes out of its ruptured body. After pages of obsessive contemplation and description, she ritually devours the cockroach, finding in it the impossible "embodiment of a prehistoric, pre-symbolic, ecstatic primal divine matter" (Camillo Penna). But this effort at communion necessarily fails. The flesh of the squashed bug is *sacred*, as Bataille might put it, because it is primordially ambivalent: it arouses both disgust and desire, at once demanding and repelling our intimate contact. We cannot touch, much less eat, this debased matter; yet we can't stop ourselves from touching and eating it. Insect life is an alien presence that we can neither assimilate nor expel. Professional exterminators know this well, and so do the best theologians and philosophers. Much ink has been spilled recently exploring Thomas Nagel's question, "what is it like to be a bat?"—or more accurately: is it possible for us to know what it's like to be a bat? But the whole discussion looks suspiciously like a replay of the old philosophical canard regarding the alleged unknowability of "other minds," only tricked out this time in postmodern drag. And in any case the bat is still a mammal, a fairly close relative of ours. That makes it all much too easy.

Wouldn't it be more relevant and useful to pose the question of radical otherness in biological terms, instead of epistemological ones? It would then become a problem, not of metaphorically entering the mind of a bat, but of literally and physically entering— or metamorphosing into—the body of a housefly. And resolving such a problem would involve the transfer, not of minds, but of DNA. What's important is not to intuit what it might be like to be another species, but to discover experimentally how actually to become one. Such is the import of David Cronenberg's film *The Fly*.

Burroughs cites Rule One of basic biologic law, rigidly enforced by the Biologic Police: "Hybrids are permitted only between closely related species and then grudgingly, the hybrids produced being always sterile." To innovate means to violate this law, to introduce alien genetic material, to assume the risks of "biologic and social chaos." But then, viruses and bacteria are doing this all the time. There's nothing new about genetic engineering; as Lynn Margulis points out, humans are only now adopting techniques that prokaryotes have already been practicing for billions of years. As for viruses, they seem just to be transposable elements—such as can be found in any genome—which have revolted against the tyranny of the organism, or otherwise gotten out of hand. From meiosis to symbiotic merger, every genetic recombination is a new throw of the dice. No such process can be controlled or determined in advance. In Cronenberg's film, *Homo sapiens* meets *Musca domestica* only by the sheerest contingency. The transformation of Seth Brundle (Jeff Goldblum) into an insect—more precisely, into the monstrous hybrid Brundlefly—is a statistical aberration: an improbable accident, a fortuitous encounter, an irreproducible singular event. That's why Seth never quite comprehends what is happening to him, at least not at the moment that it happens. His scientific consciousness lags perpetually behind his ceaselessly mutating body. His theories about his condition are out of date by the time he utters them. Cronenberg's human-turned-fly is the post-modern realization of Nietzsche's prophecy of the Overman: "man is something that should be overcome." For the *Ubermensch* is not the "higher man," nor is he any sort of fixed entity. Rather he is a perpetual becoming, an ungrounded projection into unknowable futurity. The singular hybrid Brundlefly is just such a body, without stable identity, caught in the throes of transformation. Did Nietzsche ever suspect that his great metaphysical longing would be most compellingly realized in insect form? Any scientist can make observations about how flies (or bats, or humans) act in general; but even Seth Brundle never *knows* from the inside "what it's like" to be a fly. For "what it's like" necessarily involves the irreversible *othering* of the knower: the "going-under" of the Overman, the continual "becoming" of Brundlefly. The pursuit of knowledge, as Foucault puts it, should result not just in the "acquisition of things known," but above all in "the going-astray of the one who knows."

Insects are well ahead of humans in this regard. Radical becomings take place routinely in their own lives. This is especially so in groups that pass through pupal metamorphosis. Their bodies are broken down and completely rebuilt in the course of transmutation from the larval to the mature stage. Is the butterfly "at one" with the caterpillar? Is this housefly buzzing around my head "the same" as the maggot it used to be? One genome, one continuously replenished body, one discretely bounded organism; and yet a radical discontinuity both of lived experience and of physical form. The surplus value accumulation of larval feeding gives way to lavish expenditure: the extravagant coloration of the butterflies, the coprophilic copulation of houseflies and others. Insect life cycles continually affirm the possibilities of radical difference— even if ants and bees would co-opt this difference into the homogenizing mold of the State. Every insect is a "singularity without identity," in Giorgio Agamben's phrase. The fringe biologist Donald I. Williamson even goes so far as to argue that larval stages are remnants of symbiotic mergers between formerly independent organisms. But whether or not this be literally the case, Brundle's hybridization certainly opens the door to yet stranger metamorphoses. The body of an insect—far more radically than the mind of a dialectician—is perpetually "other than itself."

The high intelligence and adaptive flexibility of mammals is usually attributed to our premature birth, and consequent long period of growth outside the womb. Genetics is supplemented by empirical learning and parental guidance. We lay down numerous memory traces, and build up complex personalities. Learning doesn't play such a role in insect development: not only because they have too few neurons to store all that information, but more crucially because memory traces cannot survive intact through the vast physiological changes of pupal transmutation. We higher mammals like to congratulate ourselves on our supposed ability to alter our own behavior adaptively in the span of an single lifetime. But this complacency may well be exaggerated. Innovation is harder than it seems. Insects usually manage to adapt to changed environmental circumstances a lot faster than we do, thanks to their greater propensity to generate mutations, and their far higher rate of genetic recombination over the course of much shorter reproductive cycles. In humans and other mammals, once memory traces are forged and reinforced, it's nearly impossible to get rid of them. And as if that weren't enough, we've also instituted *traditions* and *norms of critical reflection*, the better to police our identities, and to prevent our minds and bodies from going astray. Education, after all, is just a subtler and more sadistically refined mode of operant conditioning than the one provided by direct genetic programming. As Elias Canetti remarks, no totalitarian despot can ever hope to dominate and control his subjects so utterly as human parents actually do control their children. We accept such discipline largely because we feel compensated for it by the prospect of imposing it in turn upon our own descendants. Our mammalian talents for memory and self-reflection serve largely to oppress us with the dead weight of the past. Morse Peckham is right to insist that only "cultural vandalism"—the aggressive undermining of established values through random, mindless acts of destruction—can free us from this weight, and stimulate social innovation. We humans need to push ourselves to such disruptive extremes; otherwise we have no hope of matching the insects' astonishing ability to adaptively alter their physiology and behavior in a relatively brief time. Unburdened by mammalian scruples, insects effortlessly practice the Nietzschean virtue of *active forgetting*: the adult fly doesn't remember anything the maggot once knew.

Postmodern biology is increasingly oriented towards what might be called an insect paradigm. In postmodern biotechnology, according to Donna Haraway, "no objects, spaces, or bodies are sacred in themselves; any component can be interfaced with any other if the proper standard, the proper code, can be constructed for processing signals in a common language." The organicism of romantic and modernist thought—together with its political correlate, the disciplinary "biopolitics" described so powerfully by Foucault—has given way to a new model of life processes. Postmodern bodies are neither vitalistic nor mechanistic. They are structured through principles of modular interchangeability and serial repetition; they innovate, not on the basis of pregiven criteria, but experimentally, by continual trials of selection. Arthropod body plans are especially postmodern, built as they are on multiply repeated segments, that can be fused or altered to generate new, differentiated structures. (The organic metaphors of the nineteenth century, in contrast, are idealizations of vertebrate body plans). Genetic engineering, whether carried out in the laboratory or in "nature," requires just such a modular flexibility. Stephen Jay Gould, reflecting on the astonishing variety of arthropod forms discovered in the fossils of the Burgess shale, suggests that the initial diversification of multicellular life progressed precisely in this way. Cambrian evolution seems to have taken the form of a "grabbag," mixing and matching body segments in a process much like "constructing a meal from a gigantic old-style Chinese menu: one from column A, two from B, with many columns and long lists in every column." This kind of thing doesn't much happen in macroevolution any longer; but it's still crucial on the molecular-genetic level, as Christopher Wills argues. Certain mimetic butterflies, for instance, have linked "supergene complexes" that allow them alternatively to mimic any one of a number of vastly different model species. Segmented repetition with modular variation remains the basic organizing principle of all insect genomes: hence the frequency of homeotic mutations—multiplied wings and legs, antennae transformed into legs, added or subtracted segments—in irradiated laboratory strains of *Drosophila*. Melancholy old conservatives like Jean Baudrillard fear that postmodern modular coding leads to a preprogrammed "satellitization of the real," and finally to its total "extermination." But even the slightest acquaintance with insects will convince you that—contrary to Baudrillard's claims—"the hyperrealism of simulation" allows for a far greater explosion of change, multiplicity, and sheer exuberant waste than traditional organic models of production and circulation ever did.

Haraway points out that recent developments in postmodern biology involve a radical problematization and "denaturalization" of all notions of the organism and the individual. Witness Lynn Margulis on the symbiotic basis of eukaryotic cells, Richard Dawkins on "selfish genes," parasitism, and the "extended phenotype," and Leo Buss on the multiple, variant cell lineages of mammalian immune systems. When we look at the molecular-genetic basis of life, all we can find are differences and singularities: multiple variations, competing alleles, aberrant particle distributions, unforeseeable sequence transpositions. These multiplicities never add up to anything like a distinct species identity. Postmodern biology deals not with fixed entities and types, but with recurring patterns and statistical changes in large populations—whether these be populations of genes or populations of organisms. It tends to emphasize anomalous phenomena like retroviral infections and horizontal gene transfers; in such encounters, alteration "ceases to be a hereditary filiative evolution, becoming communicative or contagious" (Deleuze and Guattari). Postmodern biology moves directly between singularities without identity and population multiplicities, without having recourse either to intervening, mediating terms, or to overarching structural orders. It rejects the "holism" formerly attributed both to the individual organism and to the larger ecosystem. Look at the mutations and transpositions haunting any genome, or observe the behavioral quirks of the cockroaches invading your apartment. You will find what Deleuze and Guattari call "molecular, intensive multiplicities, composed of particles that do not divide without changing their nature, and distances that do not vary without entering another multiplicity and that constantly construct and dismantle themselves in the course of their communications, as they cross over into each other at, beyond, or before a certain threshold."

The obsolescence of those old organicist and holistic myths opens the way to strange new social and political arrangements. In our postmodern world, the "disciplinary power" analyzed by Foucault is continually being displaced into more subtly insidious modes of oppression. The ubiquitous codes of an "informatics of domination" (Haraway) are initially deployed by government bureaucracies, and then "privatized" as the property of multinational corporations. Such flexible and universal codes, insinuating themselves within all situations by processes of continual modulation, are the hallmark of what Deleuze, taking a hint from Burroughs, calls the "society of control." Cybernetic regulation is the human equivalent of the pheromone systems that regulate all activity in an ant colony. But let's not assume that this new arrangement of power forecloses all possibilities of resistance and change. As Deleuze says, "there's no need to fear or hope, but only to look for new weapons." Seth Brundle speaks of his paradoxical desire to become "the first insect politician," suggesting the possibility of an alternative insect politics, different from the totalitarianism of ants and bees. Consider that flies, like midges and mosquitoes, tend to swarm; and that locusts periodically change form, and launch forth into mass nomadic rampages. Such insects form immense crowds without adopting rigidly hierarchical structures. Their loose aggregations offer far more attractive prospects for postmodern sociality than do the State organizations of the Hymenoptera. Insect swarms are populations in continual flux, distributing themselves randomly across a vast territory. They are altered by the very processes that bring them together, so that they can neither be isolated into separate units, nor conjoined into a higher unity. "Their relations are distances; their movements are Brownian; their quantities are intensities, differences in intensity" (Deleuze and Guattari). If postmodern power is exemplified by the informational feedback mechanisms of the "insect societies," then maybe a postmodern practice of freedom can be discovered in the uncanny experience of the insect swarms. The next time you see flies swirling over a piece of dung, reflect upon what Agamben calls the "coming community," one not grounded in identity, and "not mediated by any condition of belonging"; or upon what Blanchot calls "the unavowable community" or "the negative community" or (via Bataille) "the community of those who do not have a community."

Postmodern politics, like postmodern biology, must in any case come to grips with natural selection. The romantics and the modernists alike misconceived evolution in melioristic or moralizing terms. Even today, New Age sentimentalists search frantically for any metaphysical solace that might palliate the harshness of neo-Darwinian struggle. We hear tales of beneficent feedback mechanisms (Gregory Bateson, James Lovelock), heart-warming cooperative endeavors (Francesco Varela, Stephen Jay Gould), synchronic species progression (Rupert Sheldrake), and strange attractors at the end of history (Terence McKenna). These are all visions of a world as it were without insects, one in which change would always conform to petty bourgeois standards of niceness and comfort. Burroughs and Cronenberg know better, as do biologists like Richard Dawkins. We live, as Burroughs reminds us, in a "war universe." If we want to survive, we must avoid the facile self-deceptions of teleological explanations. Let us rather construct our "war machines" according to pragmatic, immanent, selectionist principles. Mammalian immune systems in fact already work in this way: they 'learn' to recognize and destroy enemy proteins as a result of differential reproduction rates among widely varying T cells. Similar models for the adaptive growth of neurons in the human brain—"neural selectionism" and "neural Darwinism"—have been proposed by Gerald Edelman and others. And artificial intelligence research now explores the possibilities of allowing selectional processes to operate blindly, instead of imposing predetermined algorithms. All such selectional systems are what Deleuze and Guattari call *desiring machines* or *bodies without organs*: they are not closed structures, but relational networks that "work only when they break down, and by continually breaking down." Breakdowns are inevitable, since the process of adaptation is never rapid enough to keep up with the pace of continual change. And every breakdown brings to the fore an immense reservoir of new, untapped differences and mutations: material in random variation upon which selection can operate. These selectional processes, therefore, do not guarantee us anything in advance. They do not provide for a future that will comfortingly resemble the present or the past. They do not help us to imagine how things might be better—that old utopian fantasy, much beloved of 'progressive' social critics. Rather, their political efficacy lies in this: that they actually **work** to produce differences we could not ever have imagined. They provoke innovations far stranger and more radical than anything we can conceive on our own. "I love the uncertainty of the future," as Nietzsche so stirringly wrote.

So cultivate your inner housefly or cockroach, instead of your inner child. Let selectional processes do their work of hatching alien eggs within your body. And don't imagine for a second that these remarks are merely anthropomorphizing metaphors. We can kill individual insects, as spiders do; but we can't for all that extricate ourselves from the *insect continuum* that marks life on this planet. The selectional forces that modulate insect bodies and behaviors are also restlessly at work in our own brains, shaping our neurons and even our thoughts. Does such an idea revolt you? The problem might be that we can't read insect expressions: we don't know what they are thinking, or even if they are thinking. But this is nothing but an unwarranted vertebrate physiological prejudice; after all, "insects are naturally expressionless, since they wear their skeletons on the outside" (Christopher Wills). Watch for when the insect molts, and its inner vulnerability is exposed.

We should reject all distinctions of inner and outer, as of nature and culture. How could you ever hope to separate genetic influences from environmental ones, or biology from sociology? Those social critics who think "biological" means ahistorical and unchanging—and reject naturalistic explanations on that basis—clearly don't know what they are talking about. The bizarre, irreversible contingencies of natural history and cultural history alike stand out against all endeavors to endow life with meaning, goal, or permanence. Entomology is far less essentialistic, far more open to difference and change, far more attentive to the body, than is, say, cultural critique grounded in Frankfurt School post-Marxism or in Lacanian psychoanalysis. It's still common in well-meaning academic humanist circles to loathe and despise sociobiology. But this isn't just a matter of disputing some rather dubious claims about particular aspects of human behavior. What these critics really can't forgive is sociobiology's insistence upon biological embodiment itself. It's not a question of whether this or that gender trait is actually "written in our genes," so much as it is a case of the panicky denial of evolutionary contingency, or genetic limitation, altogether. Humanistic critics of biology merely perpetuate a massive, and quite traditional, idealization of human culture: one that has long fueled delusive fantasies of redemption and transcendence, and that has served as an alibi for all sorts of controls over people's lives, and moralistic manipulations of actual human behavior. Edward O. Wilson, to the contrary, made only one real mistake when he came to systematize the discipline of sociobiology: this was his choice of ants, rather than houseflies or cockroaches, as the implicit reference point for examining "human nature." Be that as it may, entomological intuitions remain more illuminating and provocative than narrowly humanistic ones. Maurice Maeterlinck well expressed the uncanny fascination of insect life nearly a century ago: "The insect brings with him something that does not seem to belong to the customs, the morale, the psychology of our globe. One would say that it comes from another planet, more monstrous, more dynamic, more insensate, more atrocious, more infernal than ours." What has changed in this picture in the last hundred years? Only one thing. We have

come to understand that such alien splendor is precisely what
defines the cruelty and beauty of **our** world.

12. | BILL GATES

It's out there. It's hungry. It grows like a cancer. There's more of it every second. It gobbles up entrepreneurs for breakfast; only the strong survive. Thanks to personal computers and fast modems and the Internet, **INFORMATION** is circulating and expanding as never before in history. We are finally moving, as Burroughs has long urged us to do, out of time and into space: away from the teleology of what Lyotard calls "metanarratives," and into the simultaneity and fractal self-similarity of the digital matrix. "Everything is information," Rudy Rucker rhapsodizes; "the world can be resolved into digital bits, with each bit made of smaller bits. These bits form a fractal pattern in fact-space." Baudrillard's once radical thesis is now a commonplace: in our postmodern economy, the proliferation of simulacra and empty digital signs replaces the production of tangible commodities, and even the simple presence of bodies and other referential objects. As Timothy Leary says, computers are the new LSD. Why bother going out to a bar, when I can dial up LambdaMOO or FurryMUCK from the ease and comfort of my own terminal at home? There's nothing like a little virtual sex to brighten up a cold winter evening. It's only a few bucks an hour, and anonymity is guaranteed. So don't waste time fretting in front of the mirror: if you're having a bad hair day, all you need to do is delete your old description file, and write yourself a new one. McLuhan, as usual, was right: the hardware depends upon the software, and not the other way around. Microsoft is bigger business than IBM. Which reminds me of a joke I heard recently: How many Microsoft employees does it take to screw in a lightbulb? Answer: none, because Bill Gates has declared darkness the new standard. Don't worry about material conditions, they're easy enough to work around. All you have to do is slap on another layer of code. Changing the lightbulb is a hardware problem, and no concern of ours.

Information is everywhere, and everything can be transformed into information. Digital code has supplanted money as the ultimate medium of exchange: what Marx calls the universal equivalent, or what McLuhan calls the Pentecostal translator. Information is the space we move in, the air we breathe. Its very ubiquity, however, makes it hard to grasp. As McLuhan says, we tend to be unconscious of our immediate technological environment, just as a fish is unaware of being in the water. Immersed as we are in information, dependent as we are upon it, we don't really know what it *is*. Indeed, information seems rather like pornography: you know it when you see it, but you can't come up with a rigorous definition. Information is addictively fascinating, just like pornography; and both media arouse the same sort of moralistic indignation. When Baudrillard, Neil Postman, Jerry Mander, and Bill McKibben rail against the evils of contemporary electronic media, they sound like nobody so much as Catherine MacKinnon and Andrea Dworkin crusading against porn. All these critics start from a correct McLuhanesque apprehension: they understand, on some dim level, that information and pornography—like all media—are not just passive means of representation, but active forces in their own right, "extensions of man" (sic) that literally remold our bodies. McLuhan notes that "new environments inflict considerable pain on the perceiver" who has not yet adapted to their conditions or learned how to negotiate their demands. It's impossible to take seriously these arguments for the elimination of television and pornography; but I can't help being impressed by the apocalyptic fervor of the anti-porn and anti-TV crusaders, their Manichean sense of the depravity of images. Writers like Postman and Dworkin are symptomatically important. They testify unwittingly to what McLuhan calls our ingrained "rear-view-mirrorism," the conservatism and inertia of our genes and memes: "moral vehemence may provide ersatz dignity for our normal moronic behavior," McLuhan says; "the normal human condition, when faced with innovation, is that of the brainwashed idiot who tries to introduce the painfully learned responses from one situation into new situations where they apply not at all."

Such idiocy, you might say, is structurally unavoidable. All media are extensions of ourselves, yet we can never keep up with the breathless speed of their mutations and metamorphoses. There's always lag, as anyone who cruises the Internet knows all too well. This explains why, as McLuhan puts it, "the content of any medium is always the preceding medium." Information is everywhere in our postmodern economy; but the content of that information—what it *tells* us, or what it's *about*—is still the old world, the world before it was altered by microtransistors and fiber-optic cables. John Perry Barlow suggests that electronic information "is like farm produce," in that "its quality degrades rapidly both over time and in distance from the source of production." Yesterday's data, like yesterday's papers, are good only for landfill, or for wrapping fish. It's a never-ending struggle, as Bill Gates would surely tell you, to stay on top of your game, to anticipate shifts in the market, and to make sure you have all the latest upgrades. So don't waste your money on CD-ROMs, whose content is obsolete even before it gets engraved in silicon. Go out and get more RAM and a faster modem instead. Artificial Intelligence theorists couldn't be more wrong than when they try to explain machine intelligence on the model of an organism's permanent, long-term memory. As McLuhan says, the mere "storage" of data is a relic of the "old technology"; in the new electronic environment, "the real job of the computer is not retrieval, but discovery." RAM is continually being swapped, and disappears entirely when you turn the computer off; a hard disk indeed preserves data, but its most important feature is that it's indefinitely rewriteable. A better organic analogy for artificial intelligence is therefore short-term memory, which is abrupt, multiple, and discontinuous, and "includes forgetting as an active process" (Deleuze and Guattari). Continual revision is the way out of "rear-view-mirrorism," the one way that can lead, in Foucault's words, to "the going-astray of the one who knows." The greatest virtue of the computer is that it allows us more and more to dispense with long-term memory, and to approach something like Andy Warhol's state of eternally renewable short-term bliss: "I have no memory. Every day is a new day because I don't remember the day before. Every minute is like the first minute of my life . . . My mind is like a tape recorder with one button—Erase."

Maybe that's what they mean when they say that "information wants to be free." Information, like Nietzsche's will to power, is not a static entity, not a resource that can be conserved or capitalized. Use it or lose it. It is a dynamic inner differential, "the last delta-t" (Pynchon), "a difference which makes a difference" (Gregory Bateson). Just as the will to power is "a structure in which differences of potential are distributed, a constitutive dissymmetry, difference, or inequality" (Deleuze), so information is composed of reversible gradients of electronic potential and ever-changing dissymmetries of charge. It is a matter of gates and switches, of pulses and fluxes. Its oscillations may be induced chemically at synaptic thresholds, or they may be triggered by clock signals on silicon chips; in either case, the world is a construct of self-organizing and self-executing binary programs. Rucker defines the information content of any object as "the length of the shortest computer program that would answer any possible question about that object"; on this basis, he proclaims that "reality" is nothing more (or less) than "an incompressible computation by a fractal cellular automaton of inconceivable dimensions." Indeed, an extensive digital software seems at work within the most diverse regimes of matter: we find the same nonlinear equations, fractal patterns, and strange attractors regulating variations in the weather, disturbances of cardiac rhythms, distributions of charge in neural networks, fluctuations in the stock market. But these are not closed, balanced systems; they are rather what Ilya Prigogine and Isabelle Stengers call *dissipative* structures, operating in "far-from-equilibrium" conditions, forever poised at the edge of chaos. Being is not stable, but paradoxically, precariously *metastable*.

In such conditions, behavior is in a real sense spontaneous or "free": infinitely sensitive to the most minute variations, it cannot be predicted, anticipated, or controlled from the outside. Not even Marxists believe in central planning anymore. But this "free" behavior is still information, and nothing but information: which means that it *is* ultimately computable, to any desired degree of accuracy. It's simply a matter of running the right simulations: of course, you need good software, and an awful lot of CPU time. Chaos theory thus harmonizes freedom and determinism, or chance and necessity, in much the same way that Leibniz, the first great philospher of information, reconciled free will with the infallible foreknowledge of God. God knows everything that will happen to me, according to Leibniz, because that information is enveloped in the concept—or as we should say, the program—of what I am. But the running of this program, the calculation of my being, is what mathematicians call an NP-complete problem: one that apparently cannot be solved by an efficient, time-reducing algorithm. The computation is so vast that it can only take place in real time, the very time of my lived experience; and the universe itself, in its entirety, is the only computer big enough to crunch all the numbers.

You might say, then, that "reality" itself is one enormous simulation, with information continually being computed to infinite decimal places. In the beginning was not the Word, but lines and lines of code. God is neither a stern judge nor a loving father; he is rather, as Leibniz implicitly argues, a master programmer. Such is the theology best suited to our postmodern experience of the hyperreal: a vision that moves beyond the dead end of modernist paranoia. Descartes, the prototypical modernist, worried that the Deity was actually an evil demon, bent on deceiving him. His attempts to persuade himself that God could be trusted after all are never altogether convincing. For once the seeds of paranoid doubt and existential *angst* have been planted, there's no way of eradicating them. Even Baudrillard is still a Late Cartesian, worried that hyperreal simulation has left us adrift in a vacant universe, "without origin or reality." For us, however—as indeed already for Leibniz—this simply isn't a problem. The discovery that God is a programmer running simulations is precisely what guarantees his veracity. For if God wanted to deceive us, then first and foremost he'd have to deceive himself. But if that were the case, then even his lies would end up being true. As Hans Moravec puts it, "A simulated Descartes correctly deduces his own existence. It makes no difference just who or what is doing the simulation—the simulated world is complete in itself." Our existence is no less real, for being that of a computer simulation, or an idea in the mind of God. Reality-testing involves what Wittgenstein would call a *deep tautology*: "What is, is. No fantasy. Pain. Just the details" (Kathy Acker). For what other criterion of truth and reality do we have? Philosophers in the Cartesian tradition are always trying to establish foundations and universals. But in every case, the philosophical groundings they've come up with are less evident, less solid and secure, than the very phenomena they are supposed to ground. The only convincing 'reality test' is a pragmatic one: "Just try—in a real case—to doubt someone else's fear or pain" (Wittgenstein). When we say that something is "real," we generally mean that it's so vivid, overwhelming, and all-embracing that it would be a frivolous—or willfully cynical—intellectual exercise to entertain Cartesian doubts as to its validity. Something is real because it's intense, and not the reverse.

And so we no longer ask the old Cartesian question: is it real or is it Memorex? We trust and believe that the world is real, precisely *because* we know it to be a simulation. Thanks to computers, we have rid ourselves of the representationalist prejudice that played so baleful a role in the history of Western thought. For a simulation is not a representation, but something altogether different: "to simulate something you need more than mere mimicry, more than an ability to produce actions that are like the ones you are wanting to simulate. You need a working model" (Benjamin Woolley). A representation *comes after* the object it imitates or signifies. That's why "the symbol is the murder of the thing," as Lacan put it: every representation implies, to some measure, the "lack"—the replacement, the death or the absence—of the thing it is supposed to represent. A simulation, on the contrary, *precedes* its object: it doesn't imitate or stand in for a given thing, but provides a program for generating it. The simulacrum is the birth of the thing, rather than its death. As Deleuze and Guattari say, simulation is how the real is effectively produced. No real without its hyperreal: the map becomes the territory. Reality will be virtual, or not at all. We live in an age of information, rather than one of representation and signification; and information is characterized by plenitude and redundancy—not lack. Leibniz argues that, among all possible worlds, God necessarily chose to create the one having "the greatest quantity of reality." In postmodern terms, this amounts to saying that the program simulating our universe is more powerful and detailed, more intense, more packed with information—more **real**, in short—than anything we could possibly run on our own feeble machines, or imagine inside our heads. The situation is rather like that in quantum mechanics. A wave function is inherently indeterminate and probabilistic; but it collapses, or gets determined, once it has been observed and measured. Contrary to popular misconception, however, this measuring intervention need not imply consciousness on the part of the 'observer.' A mechanical device, like a counter, is sufficient to make the wave function collapse. Simulation, likewise, is a relativistic and perspectival process, but not for all that a subjective one. It coerces my participation, but does not require it. As Wallace Stevens writes, "it fills the being before the mind can think." Information overload, you might say, is our proof that an external world really exists. We do not hallucinate an imaginary presence, says Deleuze: "it's rather presence itself that is hallucinatory."

I'm drawn into this delirium every time I turn on my modem. I log in to my account, access the World Wide Web, and head out in search of information. Too much is never enough. It accumulates more and more, in a classic feedback loop. First I download a file, then I need a program to read it. Then I discover a bug in the program, so I have to look around for a patch or an upgrade. And then I'm desperate to find more files, just to make running the program worthwhile. It's like what they say about drugs: watch out for that first hit, because each step leads to the next. Better not even inhale. Before I knew it, I was hooked: now my hard drive's entirely full, and I've got to shell out for a bigger one. It's all so absorbingly self-referential; there's no end to the digital labyrinth. Pynchon sees this process as a virtual reconfiguration of the American landscape, with information space overlaid upon, and literally mapping to, the shopping malls and real estate subdivisions of suburbia: "it was like walking among matrices of a great digital computer, the zeroes and ones twinned above, hanging like balanced mobiles right and left, ahead, thick, maybe endless." On the information superhighway, every house is a byte or a pixel, and there are endless opportunities to shop. Bits, as Rucker says, are always composed of smaller bits. Leibniz similarly insists on the infinite divisibility of matter, with differences animating it on every scale. Information is always **embedded**, one level lodged inside another, sort of like the Cat in the Hat. At one extreme, digital information encompasses the entire universe. At the other extreme, the smallest possible bit is not an entity, but a difference: an on/off switch, an undecidable 1/0, an uncollapsed, still indeterminate, quantum state. Something like the **VOOM** that's in the Hat of the tiniest Cat, a force that can accomplish anything, but whose ultimate nature, says Dr. Seuss, "I never will know."

With all those levels in between, surfing the Net can be daunting. So much depends upon finding a clean, manageable interface, and a smoothly-running client program. The sheer ugliness of MS-DOS and Windows is one thing for which I never can forgive Bill Gates. There's no need for such opaque protocols and rigid hierarchies, since fractal patterns, like all those Cats in all those Hats, remain self-similar across differences of scale. In cyberspace, linear and hierarchical modes of organization are replaced by what McLuhan calls a "mosaic," or what Leo Steinberg calls a "flatbed": "the flatbed picture plane makes its symbolic allusion to hard surfaces such as tabletops, studio floors, charts, bulletin boards—any receptor surface on which objects are scattered, on which data is entered, on which information may be received, painted, impressed—whether coherently or in confusion . . . the painted surface is no longer the analogue of a visual experience of nature but of operational processes." With programs like Netscape Navigator, you can jump discontinuously from any point in the World Wide Web to any other point, without having to traverse all those tedious up-and-down intermediate links. Microsoft was way behind in adopting this paradigm. World Wide Web browsers turn the Internet into what Deleuze and Guattari call smooth or *rhizomatic* space: a space of "acentered systems, finite networks of automata in which communication runs from any neighbor to any other, the stems or channels do not preexist, and all individuals are interchangeable, defined only by their *state* at a given moment." Selves are no longer constrained by rules of unity and organic form. You can adopt whatever handle or pseudonym you want. We are all the same in cyberspace, and anyone can be replaced by anyone else, just as Andy Warhol dreamed. But the *states* that such interchangeable individuals can occupy are multiplied far beyond our preexisting, restrictive norms; on LambdaMOO, for example, ten genders are currently available, instead of merely two.

But let's not get carried away with utopian fantasies. Most straight men are assholes, and the mere opportunity for expanded gender play on the Net doesn't do anything to change *that*. A successful drag performance is harder to pull off than you might think. Straight guys often pretend to be girls on the Net—I've done it often myself—thinking that the disguise will make it easier to get attention, and especially to score with 'actual' girls. But what goes around, comes around: the girls these guys meet usually turn out to be yet other guys in virtual disguise. Face it, the information of which most straight men are composed is monotonously self-referential: it just turns round and round forever, in the selfsame endless loop. The orgy always ends in disillusionment and boredom. However much you try, you can never be promiscuous enough. Leibniz takes the universal, orgiastic *communication of bodies*, "the fact that every portion of matter is agitated by the motions of the entire universe, and is acted upon in some way by all other parts of matter, however distant," as evidence for a cosmic "pre-established harmony." He reasons that, since everything is connected, and all these connections constitute information, and all information is computable (at least ideally, in the mind of God), then we must be living in the best of all possible worlds. By a similar argument, physicists long imagined that they were on the brink of discovering a 'final theory of everything,' and that the ultimate laws of nature would turn out to make a structure of great simplicity and beauty. If only Congress hadn't cancelled funding for the Superconducting Super Collider! But let's face it, guys, the universe's actual operating system is an ugly, inelegant hodgepodge—much like MS-DOS and Windows. I vastly prefer the Macintosh operating system myself; but I know that imperfection is inherent to design, and that even the best program is less a dazzlingly logical and elegant construction than it is a heterogeneous assemblage, buggy and inconsistent, patched with dubious trade-offs and quick and dirty shortcuts. That's the only way natural selection can operate. The postmodern God, it would seem, resembles Bill Gates far more than he does Leibniz's all-wise Designer. God, like Gates, has exactly the aggressiveness, the competitive drive, and the sense of entitlement you'd expect in a talented straight boy from a privileged WASP background. He's an obsessive hacker, a brilliant but clumsy *bricoleur*, with an brute-force approach to problem-solving. He's a ferocious workaholic, who regularly puts in 80-hour weeks, and expects his employees to do the same. And although he's something of a visionary, he's not a particularly reliable one; he never meets product deadlines, and the goods he so tirelessly promotes are mostly vaporware. God, like Gates, owes his power and success less to the quality of his product than to his ruthless business sense. He's created a near monopoly by outmuscling the competition. You might not like this universe, just as you might not like Microsoft's clunky programs; but pragmatically speaking, where else do you have to go?

It's Bill Gates's world; we just live in it. Even a cursory look at Microsoft programs will disabuse you of the notion that the workings of natural selection, or of the "free market," somehow lead to optimal solutions. Most of the time, they leave us stranded, as it were, in the basins of insufficiently strange attractors: stable but suboptimal norms, programs that work just well enough to avert too frequent crashes, and to foreclose the chance of further innovation. Even God, you might say, can't *really* make the trains run on time. Information wants to be free; but its liberation won't have the glittering consequences that its proponents sometime imagine: "though at first thought a leap out of our biological bodies [and into cyberspace] might seem to free us of the diseases of the flesh—alas, it is not so" (Hans Moravec). Today's simple computer viruses are only the beginning, as Moravec almost gleefully explains. Even as I write, new strains are being reported that mutate slightly in every generation, just enough to evade detection by standard anti-virus programs. For information has a body, even if it's not always the carbon-based one we've been accustomed to. Information is never just meaning, it's never a pure signal: there's always some waste in the form of redundancy, and there's always an uneliminable residue of noise. Redundancy and noise are information's body, the excess—the nonproductive expenditure—without which it couldn't function at all. They are inherent features of the medium, which means that they take precedence over any particular message. As Michel Serres points out, in living systems the couple 'message/noise' itself becomes, on a meta-level, a new form of information. And as Prigogine and Stengers observe, for living systems "a random fluctuation in the external flux, often termed 'noise,' far from being a nuisance, produces new types of behavior." So let's stammer and stutter and repeat ourselves, spam the terminals, jam the channels, and otherwise revel in information overload. The problem with Microsoft software isn't so much that it's heavy and slow, and filled with bugs and redundancies. What's truly obnoxious about it is that in spite of its flaws, it functions all too slickly and too well. It establishes a field of coherence and closure that reins in excess, and shuts out other programs. The problem is not with Bill Gates the hacker, but with Bill Gates the monopolist who unilaterally imposes the latest standard.

So think again about that lightbulb that Gates couldn't be troubled to screw in. "The electric light is pure information," says McLuhan; "it is a medium without a message, as it were, unless it is used to spell out some verbal ad or name." The sheer dissipation of the lightbulb, its prodigal display of luminescence, its irreversible expenditure of itself in heat: this is a delirium of pure information. You could stare at that one bulb for hours, in a psychedelic trance. Of course someone will always try to use the lightbulb, to get some reading done, to sell some product, or to spell out some illustrious name. But the Second Law of Thermodynamics assures us that information cannot ever entirely be put to work. The medium is more than the sum of its messages and uses. Information is ecstatic, before it is communicative. It will be convulsive, or not at all. Remember Pynchon's story of Byron the Bulb, the lightbulb that burns forever? The international electronics cartel, concerned for its bottom line, sends out hit squads to 'retire' him. But Byron is effectively immortal; somehow he escapes each time, and continues to be screwed into socket after socket. Byron the Bulb embodies information in its pure state, sterile and sublime and incommunicable, unable to be accounted for, never to be put to any productive use: "he is condemned to go on forever, knowing the truth and powerless to change anything." And indeed one day "he will find himself, poor perverse bulb, enjoying it . . ."

So there you have it. Turn on, tune in, drop out. In this new world of electronic information, it's not what you know that is important, but the fact that, whatever it is, and wherever it comes from, it just never stops. That's the real point behind Leary's claim that netsurfing and virtual reality extend the effects of LSD by other means. It's not that you receive any profound new revelations when you're tripping; if you think you do, as often happens, you're only fooling yourself. But the value of psychedelia is that it *is* a vertigo of redundancy, an ecstasy of sheer quantitative overload. It's a feedback effect, like playing an electric guitar right up against the speakers. The message itself is unimportant. What really changes, thanks to the blast of these interference patterns, is the medium, or the messenger. All media, McLuhan says, are prosthetic implants, extensions of ourselves. But don't imagine that you can extend yourself with impunity, without being deeply changed by the experience. Even if you are just sitting there stooped over your terminal, or off in a corner, in a drug-induced stupor, staring at a lightbulb and muttering to yourself—even then, or rather especially then, you will hear voices that are profoundly alien. Terence McKenna calls them elves and pixies, William Gibson Haitian loas, Burroughs brain parasites from Venus, Jack Spicer little green men from Mars, John Carpenter free marketeers from Andromeda. Whatever. These beings may be malicious, or simply indifferent to us. They probably don't have our best interests at heart. But who cares where they come from, or even what they want? It's not as if we could make them go away; it's far too late for that. We have to learn to live with them; there's no other option. In the words of Sun Ra and his Intergalactic Solar Arkestra: "It's after the end of the world. Don't you know that yet?"

13. PAVEL CURTIS

Maybe it happens like this. You are sitting at a cluttered desk, in a stuffy, dimly lit room, somewhere in Seattle. It's night. It's very late. Everyone else must be asleep by now. If you leaned out the window to take in a breath of fresh air, you might see Jupiter and Mars gleaming in the constellation Scorpio. But the window is closed, and the shades are drawn. You are sitting in an uncomfortable office chair, hunched over a small terminal. Despite the awkward posture and the stifling atmosphere, you remain just as you are; you don't even consider getting up. Modem lights blink, the hard drive whirs, lines of text scroll across the screen. Occasionally, there is a loud beep. Your eyes squint at the small print; your fingers move frantically across the keyboard. You notice you've made a typo, and groan in disgust. Meanwhile, new incoming messages keep on arriving. You feel a sense of hysterical overload, as your brain strives to process five separate trains of thought at once. You're wondering how much longer you can keep it up, addressing your replies correctly, typing all those puns and sly allusions and heartfelt pleas and properly formatted commands, while at the same time reading the incoming lines as quickly as possible, before they scroll off the top of the screen. Until, all of a sudden, you hit a lag. None of your commands are executed, and nobody else's input appears on your terminal. Twenty-five seconds that seem like an eternity, as you wait impatiently for something—anything—to happen. Frustrated, irritated, you wonder if this isn't the time to call it a night. But you know that if you quit now, a vague sense of dissatisfaction would linger, and you'd never be able to fall asleep.

Or maybe it happens like this. You've been wandering for hours through the Lambda mansion and its luxurious grounds. You took a swim in the pool, grabbed a snack in the kitchen, read some books in the library, and fell through a mirror into a dingy old tavern. You entered an alien spacecraft, and fiddled around with the controls. You wandered through the cubes of a tesseract, trying to work out the geometry of its intrusion into three-space. You tried your luck in a gambling arcade, and lost all your money at the video slot machines. You climbed a rose trellis and found yourself on the roof of the mansion; you took in a breath of fresh night air, and saw Jupiter and Mars gleaming in the constellation Scorpio. Now you're sitting in a hot tub, sipping a beer, trying to relax and think about it all. But things have only gotten faster and more frantic. Close to twenty people are packed into this one space. You feel a sense of hysterical overload, as you try to follow five separate conversations at once. It's hard even to keep track of your companions, as their names keep changing, while their bodies metamorphose from one gender to another. Some dude is playing power chords on his guitar; another is inhaling outrageous tokes from a seven-foot-tall bong. A helicopter buzzes overhead; the pilot leans out and waves. This one jerk keeps whispering dumb pick-up lines and sexual insinuations into your ear. Someone else dunks you under the water, just for fun. Meanwhile, you're trying halfheartedly to flirt, in hurried whispers, with this cute guy you've just met. Until, all of a sudden, you hit a lag. Everyone seems to have gone into a catatonic stupor. Twenty-five seconds that seem like an eternity, as you wait impatiently for something—anything—

to happen. Frustrated, irritated, you wonder if this isn't the time to call it a night. But you know that if you went home now, a vague sense of dissatisfaction would linger, and you'd never be able to fall asleep.

Just another evening at LambdaMOO. Two alternative descriptions of the same series of events. But whose life is this, anyway? What does it mean to say that I was simultaneously here and there, both wandering the grounds of LambdaMOO and sitting quietly at home? Just what kind of a place is a text-based virtual world? Is the landscape of a MUD or a MUCK or a MOO somehow more **real** than that of a novel or a movie or a sexual fantasy or a Sega video game? Or must I concede that the first of my descriptions— sitting in front of the terminal—is literal, material, embodied, and actual, while the other—lounging in the hot tub—is merely fictive, figurative, disembodied, and imaginary? Then RL ("real life") would be to VR ("virtual reality") as experience is to its mimetic representation. Or as an author (or a reader?) is to a fictional character. Or as the physical body is to the body in Freudian fantasy. Or as what semioticians call the "subject of the enunciation" is to what they call the "subject of the statement." How else could one possibly make sense of all this?

But when you're caught up in the vertigo of MUDs and MOOs, such distinctions no longer make sense. Try it yourself if you don't believe me. Spend some time in a virtual world, and you'll be amazed how real it can be. We fight, we fuck, we sing and dance, we take drugs: "though initially loosing consciousness from matter, MUDs end up producing a curious twin body, a doppelgänger that explores, wrestles, hugs, and laughs" (Erik Davis). Total strangers become intimate friends or lovers, almost overnight. Jealousies develop, and quarrels break out, followed by mutual avoidance, or by tearful reconciliations. The sense of tactile, corporeal presence, throughout it all, is overwhelming. Yes, that was indeed my body, sweating, grunting, straining its eyes, furiously typing. But that was also my body, relaxing in the hot tub, drinking a beer, splashing, casually flirting, sorting out sexual responses, and reeling off lame one-liners. All these events occurred together, in real time, in the same stream of consciousness, along the same continuum of bodily sensations. I got tipsy on that virtual beer; the warmth of the water in the hot tub merged with the stifling heat of the air in my study. For reality is a matter, not of essences, but of effects; my actions have continuing reverberations and consequences in Lambda-MOO, just as they do in RL. Deleuze writes of a hallucinatory "excess of presence, that acts directly on the nervous system, and that makes representation—with its putting-in-place or putting-at-a-distance—impossible." In this sense, LambdaMOO is a fully present, actual world—and not just a vicarious representation of one. For all that it's made out of binary code in a mainframe and words scrolling on a screen, LambdaMOO is as vividly concrete and detailed as the room from which I access it, and as engaging and crowded, as friendly or as menacing, as the bar down the street.

At LambdaMOO, we like to talk about the differences—but that also means the solidarities—between VR and RL. One doesn't exist without the other. Indeed, it gets tricky at times. Each player on the MOO has eir own pseudonym or 'handle': so that unless you choose to tell me, there's no way I can find out who you 'really' are. Anyone you meet online is playing a role, adopting a persona; but isn't that the case when we meet in RL as well? It's not that I know you less well in VR, but that I come to know you in a radically different way. I may become quite intimate with someone, spend hours with em every night, and yet not have the slightest idea what eir voice sounds like, or what eir RL body looks, feels, and smells like. Thanks to pseudonymity, the space for deception may well be larger in VR than in RL. But the space for experimentation, invention, and discovery is also larger, by the same logic. Inhibitions are lowered; the most unlikely and unexpected patterns emerge. "Erotic interaction in cyberspace," as Shannon McRae puts it, "requires a constant phasing between the virtual and the actual, the simultaneous awareness of the corporeal body at the keyboard, the emoting, speaking self on the screen, and the existence of another individual, real and projected, who is similarly engaged. Far from producing a mind-body split that allows for the projection of an intact ego, self-awareness must be doubled, multiplied, magnified, to an extent that the 'self' is rendered incoherent, scattered, shattered." Are all these exciting and excruciating transformations 'real'? You'd better believe it.

Or take, as another example, the phenomenon of lag: a perpetual annoyance to every MOOer. Too many people are logged in, trying to execute too many commands at once: the server at Xerox PARC is overloaded. Even in the electronic global village, sometimes you just have to wait. Lag is clearly an event in RL, caused by the physical condition of the hardware. It happens as I sit in front of my monitor, waiting for more lines to scroll. But lag is also integral to VR: not a limitation upon it, so much as an aspect of it, something woven into its very texture. Lag is a feature of my VR life, even as incessant rain is a part of my RL in Seattle. There's a lag-meter in the Lambda living room, just as there's a barometer in my Seattle living room. As legba said the other night, we even talk about lag in LambdaMOO in much the same way we talk about the weather in RL. *Virtual*, then, does not mean 'imaginary' or 'unreal.' As Deleuze says, the virtual is altogether real in its own way; it should never be confused with the merely 'possible.' Indeed, philosophically speaking, 'virtual' and 'possible' are almost opposites. The imaginary and the unreal are subsets of the possible. A logically impossible object, like a square circle, cannot strictly speaking be imagined. On the other hand, whatever we *can* imagine is possible, no matter how unreal. Teleportation, for instance, is easily imaginable in RL, and hence possible, although the technological difficulties in making it work are probably insurmountable. But things are quite different in VR. Here, teleportation is an actual fact, not something you imagine. After all, it makes no difference to the LambdaMOO database whether I walk out from the hot tub onto the deck, or transport myself directly from the hot tub to the library. Objects in VR, then, are real and impossible, instead of being unreal and possible. They are not fantasy representations; they are simply more fluid, more open to mutation and metamorphosis, than their RL counterparts. After I left the hot tub, I stared at a painting in the library, trying to scrutinize the details of its brushwork. Before I knew it I was *inside the painting*, transported into another world. I was alone. The scene was bucolic, yet an unspoken feeling of menace floated almost palpably in the air . . . As in an H. P. Lovecraft story, I can't quite remember what happened next, nor do I recall just how I finally escaped. But like the narrator of a Lovecraft story, I remain firmly convinced that it all really happened, even though the physical evidence has somehow mysteriously disappeared.

Michael Heim traces the term *virtual* back to Duns Scotus, who used it "to bridge the gap between formally unified reality (as defined by our conceptual expectations) and our messily diverse experiences." Virtual Reality, you might say, is the actual mode of being of the inessential, the epiphenomenal, and the non-conceptual: of all that is unpredictable, unexpected, transitory, contingent, or exceptional. VR is then not metaphysical, but 'pataphysical. We imagine and represent unreal possibilities, but the real itself, in its messy diversity, is unrepresentable and unimaginable. To paraphrase Sherlock Holmes: once you've eliminated the possible (that is to say, everything that can be imagined, but that doesn't really exist) then the virtual, however improbable or outrageous, is what remains. VR thus includes those anomalous *quasi-existences* painstakingly catalogued by Charles Fort: rains of blood, strange hybrids, stigmata, spontaneously combusting bodies, perpetual motion machines, poltergeist girls, falls of fishes from the sky. But VR also includes everything that is banal, everyday, and boringly unremarkable: the "nine tenths" of our life that goes on without will or conscious thought (Robert Bresson), the "dirt under the fingernails" for which a Platonic Idea is lacking (Deleuze). Such a combination of the remarkable and the insignificant, the singular and the trivial, is familiar to anyone who hangs out in MUDs and MOOs. We might do well to adopt the logic of Fort's research program for our own postmodern explorations of virtual worlds: "there is, in quasi-existence, nothing but the preposterous—or something intermediate to absolute preposterousness and final reasonableness . . . Infinite frustrations of attempts to positivize manifest themselves in infinite heterogeneity: so that though things try to localize homogeneousness they end up in heterogeneity so great that it amounts to infinite dispersion or indistinguishability."

Life in LambdaMOO is just such a quasi-existence. Far from being an imaginary, mental structure, it is actively composed of precisely those things the mind is unable to grasp. I'm continually blown away by LambdaMOO's "excess of presence," meaning both its psychedelic 'too-muchness' (what Deleuze would call its "intensity") and its ungrounded superfluousness (what Fort would call its preposterous "externality"). We attempt to homogenize this experience, but we are continually thrown back upon Fort's "infinite dispersion," or upon what William Gibson calls the "unthinkable complexity" of the Matrix. Gibson defines cyberspace, or any form of VR, as a "consensual hallucination." Both words in this definition merit extended comment. LambdaMOO is indeed a hallucination, a simulacral construct; but then again, so is everything else that we perceive or experience as "real." To encounter the real, as Nietzsche says, is to be "necessitated to error." The senses themselves "do not lie"; but "what we *make* of their testimony . . . introduces lies." The direct, intense stimulation of my sensory neurons provokes the construction of elaborate simulations in the perceptual centers of my brain. And it is these simulations, in turn, that endow external objects with their ring of authenticity and truth, and that guide and facilitate my bodily engagement in the world. Awake or asleep, we are always simulating and hallucinating. This doesn't mean that reality is a somehow a product of our minds. On the contrary: we are bound to hallucination, necessitated to error, exactly to the extent that reality is objective and external: inescapable in its presence, yet irreducible to our representations and refractory to our desires. Like it or not, it's *there*. Thought is never spontaneous; it requires a body to provoke it and (as Lyotard says) to make it suffer. Even in VR, objects have a definite existential integrity: they are more dense and solid, more user- and perceiver-independent—more *objective* in short—than you would ever imagine. For a postmodern sensibility, the world is a fictional construct, not in spite of its apparent presence and immediacy, but precisely *because* of these. Excess, delirium, anxiety, sublimity, preposterousness, undecidability, the *mise en abîme* of binary oppositions, the breakdown of representational order: these are all consequences— or better, hi-tech "special effects"—of presence itself, and not (as the deconstructionists too simply suppose) of the critique or deferral of presence.

So you could say that my RL apartment in Seattle depends upon a "consensual hallucination," every bit as much as do such virtual, abstract entities as subatomic particles, the American legal system, and LambdaMOO. In all these cases, the hallucination is shared, public, and objective, just because it is consensual. As Wittgenstein insisted, there is no such thing as a private language. Even your fantasies, dreams, and inner psychotic delusions must forcibly be rendered into the dominant reality. Gibson's word *consensual* implies a constraint far stronger, and far more sinister, than the mere legal notion of a formal acceptance by all parties. It's more like what the Mafia calls "an offer you can't refuse." The ultimate proof that something is "real" is that it imperiously demands my assent at every moment. Seattle and LambdaMOO both exist independently of my will; it's for that very reason that I am required to torture my will into conformity with them. As Guattari once said, politics precedes ontology. The exercise of power, according to Foucault, is "a set of actions upon other actions . . . it is always a way of acting upon an acting subject or acting subjects by virtue of their acting or being capable of action." That is to say, power always implies the separation or "freedom" of its victim. This is what behaviorist psychology was never able to grasp. It isn't enough that I am "determined" by the "laws" of nature, or culture, or language. No, I also must be led (induced, seduced, coerced, cajoled) into giving my "free" consent to all of these laws. Just as workers in service industries today can't get away simply with performing their tasks efficiently; they are also required to exude team spirit, and to grovel and smile obsequiously before their customers. It's an old story: you encounter it everywhere, from software licensing agreements to social contract theories. Merely by opening the package and removing the disk, you've agreed to all sorts of dubious contractual obligations. You may not like them, but your consent is the price you must pay in order to be able to run a computer in the first place. Similarly, social contract theories (and their more recent descendants, like Lacan's account of the Symbolic order) tell you that, simply by virtue of being a functioning member of society, you have freely consented to abrogate your own freedom. But of course, there's no alternative to this freely willed choice: for it's only insofar as you are a socially constituted being that you have the occasion and ability to make free choices at all. Catch-22. And so it goes with everything real: withholding consent simply isn't an option. We are always collaborating in the construction of our own prisons, straining our imaginations in thrall to the dictatorship of the real. Even suicide, as Blanchot sadly notes, is still an exertion of the will, still a consensual affirmation of reality. The deaths of Kleist and of Kurt Cobain—painfully honest as these acts may have been, beautiful protests against the tyranny of the real—alas only ensured that their authors would continue to be abusively misunderstood.

VR offers us no escape from this tyranny: it's far too real for that. Virtual worlds are anchored by a concrete sense of place: in this they are utterly different from utopias, which literally are nowhere. However idealistic their programmers' intentions, MUDs and MOOs always seem to end up reinventing the bad old RL power relations. Cliques spring up, social classes develop, unequal privileges accrue, tricksters run scams, boys act just like boys, and some players have even been raped. Why am I not surprised? It reminds me of some graffiti I once read, in those old days before the Internet, when VR could only be attained through drugs: "Reality is a crutch."—"And fantasy is a broken leg." Think of VR as a kind of prosthetic device. I use my computer to talk and to listen, to feel and to touch, just as I use my eyeglasses to see. Electronic circuitry, as McLuhan says, is "an extension of the central nervous system," even as "the wheel is an extension of the foot, the book is an extension of the eye, and clothing is an extension of the skin." Virtual worlds are best understood as what

Foucault calls *heterotopias*: other-spaces, or spaces of otherness, in contrast to utopian non-spaces. "The mirror is, after all, a utopia, since it is a placeless place . . . But it is also a heterotopia insofar as the mirror does exist in reality, where it exerts a sort of counteraction on the position that I occupy . . . The mirror functions as a heterotopia in this respect: it makes this place that I occupy at the moment when I look at myself in the glass at once absolutely real, connected with the space that surrounds it, and absolutely unreal, since in order to be perceived it has to pass through this virtual point which is over there." Heterotopias, unlike utopias, have bulk, weight, and friction; they are never exempt from the power relations and constraints of the societies that spawn them. Indeed, heterotopias express these relations and constraints even to excess: they are "capable of juxtaposing in a single real place several spaces, several sites that are in themselves incompatible." But in so doing, they map out points of fracture in the fabric of their culture; they twist the social forms of which they are composed into strange new ungainly shapes.

Foucault cites pirate ships and brothels as exemplary instances of heterotopia in modern Western culture: virtual spaces, as it were, for a time before computers. (It's no accident, I think, that such spaces play so prominent a role in the brilliantly subversive novels of Kathy Acker). May not VR, with its shifting subjectivities, its incompatible juxtapositions, its nomadic displacements, its piratical hackers, and its surprisingly intense netsex, become just such a space of messy, risky cultural innovation? Not utopian social engineering, but experimentation and *bricolage*—with all the silly and obnoxious, as well as useful and beautiful, consequences that may ensue. Pavel Curtis, the chief programmer and wizard (system administrator) of LambdaMOO, urges anthropologists and sociologists to study MUDs and MOOs as prototypes of new forms of social interaction. And that's only the beginning. Allucquere Rosanne Stone foresees, in the not too distant future, a proliferation of MUDs and MOOs "in which the objects talk to each other and evolve in a Darwinian way even when no biologically based people are logged in." As VR extends and accelerates our perceptions, it may well foster the evolution of new sense organs that change our sense of being in the world so radically, that we can no longer recognize them as our own. But there's no stopping it, in any case; we are all already cyborgs, as Donna Haraway reminds us. So we may as well strap on our prostheses, and join the party.

Here's how Foucault describes the heterotopia of the pirate ship: "a floating piece of space, a place without a place, that exists by itself, that is closed in on itself and at the same time is given over to the infinity of the sea; and from port to port, from tack to tack, from brothel to brothel, it goes as far as the colonies in search of the most precious treasures they conceal in their gardens . . . The ship is the heterotopia *par excellence*. In civilizations without boats, dreams dry up, espionage takes the place of adventure, and the police take the place of pirates." In a time when, as Acker also writes, dreams have withered, and it seems no longer possible to be a pirate, isn't such *heterotopic longing* the real driving force behind our passionate embrace of VR? The space of piracy, as Foucault charts it, has a paradoxical structure. On one hand, it is intensely private, like the space of dreams: it is separated, closed off, and self-contained. But on the other hand, it is at the same time amazingly open: it enters into direct contact with infinitude, with the Outside, with the furthest reaches of the Universe. The pirate ship's very excess of closure detaches it from its initial context, and gives it an unlimited freedom to wander and explore. As Deleuze says, explicating Foucault, "an inside deeper than any internal world" immediately encounters "an outside more distant than any external world." There's no mediation here, no middle term reconciling or linking the extremes. Isn't this very much like what Mark Dery oxymoronically calls the "interactive autism" of VR? I shut myself in my room, I lock the door; I am all alone, with only a computer and a modem for company. But this privacy allows me to explore the secret gardens and brothels of cyberspace, to glean the rarest fruits and make the most intimate contacts. And that's how my body can find itself in two (or more) places at once. Michael Heim similarly describes "the erotic ontology of cyberspace" in terms taken from Leibniz: "monads have no windows, but they do have terminals." Every monad is a world unto itself, "an independent point of vital willpower"; no common space unites them, and they "never meet face-to-face." But don't think of this as some sort of alienation or absence; for the absolute closure of each monad is precisely what allows them all to be online together, in the same virtual space, on the same network. "In electric systems," as McLuhan puts it, "communication is by gaps, switches, and transistors." Sparks fly across synapses and through logic gates. We have scarcely begun to explore the erotics of these sparks, these transfers, the compelling immediacy and intimacy of contact at a distance.

The pirate ship's nomadic trajectory, like that of the MUD dweller or the Internet voyager, rips apart the fabric of linear, homogeneous, visual, perspectival space. We move, as McLuhan says, into a space that has become audile-tactile instead of visual: interactive, simultaneous, heterogeneous, discontinuous, multi-directional, diversely textured. MUDs and MOOs, at this point, are still text-based and low-bandwidth; but as Curtis argues, that only makes them "cooler" as a medium, more inclusive, participatory, and tactile. As the phonetic alphabet scrolls rapidly across my screen, it at long last loses the tyrannical privilege that it has possessed since Gutenberg. For "language was the last art to accept the visual logic of Gutenberg technology, and the first to rebound in the electric age" (McLuhan). I learn to read and write in a new way, one more suited to a postmodern, postliterate culture. New habits gradually form, new perceptions, new sexual kinks. Every new medium, as McLuhan says, "affects physiology as well as psychic life." We feel sensations in our prostheses, just as amputees do in phantom limbs. Yes, that was me you saw at LambdaMOO the other night. And as my @description file must have told you, I was awake and looked alert.

14. TRUDDI CHASE

The abuse started when you were very young, perhaps only two years old. At least that's what somebody locked deep inside you remembers. Confined spaces in which the (step)father imprisoned you, his sweaty, stinking bulk manhandling and penetrating your flesh. The memory is indubitable, vividly real, even if it isn't precisely your own. You bear the scars to this day. How inadequate to reduce it to some merely Symbolic process, the Law of the Father or whatever, when what the Republicans call *family values* are thus incised directly in female flesh. "Daddy taught me to live in pain, to know there's nothing else" (Kathy Acker). Incest and child molestation are as American as apple pie. Or should I rather say cherry pie, the dessert of choice in David Lynch's *Twin Peaks?* Leland Palmer is the all-American Dad if there ever was one, so it's more than appropriate that he is the one to be possessed by the evil spirit BOB, and to rape and murder his daughter Laura. This deed is necessarily something of a ritual, the founding gesture of the American nuclear family. "A ritual includes the letting of blood. Rituals which fail in this requirement are but mock rituals"

(Cormac McCarthy). The American nuclear family is never secure, never in place once and for all; the patriarchal pact needs continually to be renewed with vampiric infusions of fresh blood. And so "it is happening again": lookalike Maddy Ferguson takes the place of her cousin Laura Palmer, to be murdered by Leland/ BOB in her own turn. This eerie soap opera repetition is the postmodern equivalent of Freud's Primal Scene, or of Nietzsche's Eternal Return. We are all the products of such rituals, survivors of our own deaths. Every birth, every coming to awareness, occurs in excruciating pain. *When Rabbit Howls*, by The Troops for Truddi Chase, is the autobiography of an incest victim who is thus "born" all too many times: she develops multiple personalities, ninety-two distinct selves, in response to repeated parental violation. Patti Davis similarly recounts the traumatic abuse inflicted upon her by her kindly and universally revered parents, Ronald and Nancy Reagan.

The "I" is always an other, as Rimbaud said long ago. We are continually being violated in the flesh, and possessed in the spirit, by voices or by demons. Multiple Personality Disorder was once a rare and ignored condition; it suddenly became prominent just around the time Reagan was elected President. Today, it is the best paradigm we have for postmodern consciousness. No wonder it is so prominent on Oprah and Geraldo. Identity is always a multiplicity; the true first person is the plural. In Truddi Chase, an extreme case, there are 92 of "us"; in Crazy Jane, the superhero in **DOOM PATROL** who is explicitly modeled upon Truddi Chase, there are 64. But every human body contains at least one—and therefore necessarily more than one—of these multiple, incomplete selves. In the Troops that constitute Truddi Chase, each person is a closed box, a unique entity, shut off from the others. Each self has its own typical bodily gestures and facial expressions, its own particular habits, preferences, and speech patterns, and even its own pulse rate. There's the workaholic businesswoman Ten-Four, the party girl Elvira, the Barbie-like Miss Wonderful, the catatonically calm Grace, the sophisticated Catherine, the violently obscene Sewer Mouth. There are also many selves defined more by their tasks than by their emotional characteristics: the Gatekeeper, the Buffer, the Weaver, the Interpreter. But even though each of these selves is well-bounded and distinct, none is able to subsist alone. Truddi Chase's subjectivity can't be located in any one place. It is the result of an immense collaborative effort; it involves the delegation of powers, and the coordination of numerous limited and largely autonomous functions. There are memory blanks and discontinuities, as each of the selves is conscious only part of the time, and none is ever directly aware of what happens to the others. Someone acts, someone else hides in terror, someone else stirs uneasily in her sleep, and yet someone else's rage or grief is a murmur indistinctly resounding. Truddi Chase hears arguments and conversations, as if a big cocktail party were continually going on in her brain. Opaque walls divide the selves from one another, and these walls are never broken down. But disturbing moans and shouts pass through the walls, a prisoners' code alerting the selves to one another. Signals, commands, and complaints circulate among them. The multiple selves cannot ever merge into one, but they also cannot escape each other's proximity. This relation-in-difference impels their frenetic activity. The traffic is intense. With so many persons continually coming and going, Truddi Chase's hyperactive neurons are always firing, and propagating a powerful electromagnetic field. Radio, TV, and telephone transmissions are jammed with static; electrical appliances tend to malfunction in her vicinity. But if Truddi Chase has more selves and generates more interference than do most of us, the difference is only one of degree, not of kind. I am only a self in relation to another self, *in communication with another self*; I can't be *one*, without first being at least two.

Pierre Klossowski suggests that Tertullian's demonology offers a better model than does Freudian metapsychology for explaining such communication, and for conceiving multiple selves. For Freud's self-proclaimed "Copernican revolution" in psychology doesn't reject Cartesian dualism, so much as it reinscribes it by (re-)locating the ego in what still remains an exclusively interior and representational space. The ego/earth is no longer the center,

Freud says, since it is now understood to rotate around the unconscious/sun. Yet Descartes himself had already said as much, when he made the truth of the *cogito* contingent upon the ontologically prior idea of infinity or of God. For Descartes as much as for Freud, the conscious ego isn't really the center; for Freud as much as for Descartes, the integrity of self-consciousness and the privacy of mental space are paradoxically preserved by this very decentering. Freud's unconscious and Descartes' God are both structures whose infinitude escapes the ego's grasp. I can never encounter God or the unconscious directly; but the effects of their actions are so patent that I cannot doubt their existence. God and the unconscious alike absolutely exceed my powers of representation; but this very transcendence grounds and guarantees the order of mental representations. In Freud as in Descartes, then, I remain trapped within a closed circle of solipsistic self-reference; I never make the leap from mind to brain, and I never encounter anything like a body. Any surplus, any radical difference, any remainder irreducible to representation, is easily neutralized by being referred to that mythical grand Other that is God or the unconscious. Despite everything, Freud still subscribes to the relentless project, of privatizing the inner self and objectifying the outside world, that has obsessed Western culture at least since Descartes.

Klossowski, to the contrary, affirms the radical *exteriority* of psychic forces. Demonology, far better than metapsychology, recognizes that the mind is *not* its own place, with its own laws and its own order of representations. The mind is rather a sort of no man's land, a vessel for spirits, a space continually being invaded and contested by alien powers. "The woman" who *is* Truddi Chase, the self who appears continuously to others and who serves as her legal representative in the world, is just such an empty space. She is merely a puppet or a robot, a "facade," manipulated and ventriloquized by the other selves. She remembers nothing, and she speaks only from dictation, like the narrators of Beckett's fiction: as the other selves say repeatedly, "the woman can talk, but she can't think." Her identity consists only of one redundant, incessantly repeated phrase: "for you, there is nothing more." This self is entirely vacuous, yet it is necessary, for it provides the physical location that all the other selves strive to occupy. Thought is thus radically corporeal: I think when demons take hold of my body, just as BOB acts by manifesting himself in Leland's body, just as many selves inhabit the body designated as Truddi Chase. My body is alarmingly porous; it is always being penetrated, violated, and possessed. I am endowed with consciousness only to the extent that others are conscious through me.

In such circumstances, Tertullian's *credo quia absurdum* is a salutary antidote to Descartes' *cogito ergo sum*. The real is the impossible, as Lacan says. The secret of self-consciousness is that of Lewis Carroll's White Queen, who taught herself to "believe as many as six impossible things before breakfast." To affirm the reality of demonic possession is to reject the mentalist cliché (stated in its most extreme form by Bishop Berkeley, but substantially subscribed to by Freud and Lacan as well) that I can never encounter the real, because I only experience my own representations of things, and not the things themselves. The mistake of Western metaphysics since Descartes is to conceive perception and affectivity as cognitive states, and therefore to subject them to canons of representation. But sensation and emotion are visceral processes before they are intellectual ones; they are not fixed attainments of knowledge and understanding, but ongoing movements of vulnerability and arousal. Affliction precedes and exceeds awareness. When I am invested by a demon, or when I am bombarded by sensation, I am affected directly: I am seized and agitated by something that yet remains apart from me and is not accessible to my powers of representation. My very being is altered; the "I" of the previous sentence is already someone else. The conditions of possibility or forms of representation that philosophers traditionally invoke to describe my experience of, and inherence in, the world have always already been radically breached.

This *limit-experience* might seem to be a rare, extraordinary occurrence; but in fact it happens every day. I could only be a fixed self, with a unique, unchanging identity, if I were never to act, never to desire, never to experience anything new. The God of monotheism indeed sees souls in this way, *sub specie aeternitatis*. For he exists just to absorb and neutralize excess; as Schreber puts it, he only understands corpses, not living beings. But the god of *this* world is not the monotheistic one; he is rather the Baphomet, the "prince of modifications." As Klossowski explains, the Baphomet presides over an unstable and polycentric universe, an anarchy of metamorphosis and metempsychosis. William Burroughs maintains the regulative principle that we must regard every event as being willed by some agency, as being the expression of an intention. Klossowski proposes a complementary principle: he suggests that every intention is an external event, a modification of my being, and hence a sort of demonic possession. Each thought or desire is an alteration of my previous state; it is an intrusion of the outside, a whispering in my ear, a breath that I inhale and exhale, an alien spirit prompting me from offstage or insinuating itself within me. Of course, not all intentions are carried through to their conclusions; but any intention is already in itself a kind of action, a tribute paid to the Baphomet, the manifestation of some force in facial expressions and in gestures and postures of the body. Klossowski loves to depict the play of conflicting impulses as they traverse the flesh: Roberte invites the attention of some young stud by languidly proffering one upturned palm, even as her other hand irritatedly pushes him away. Analogous bodily modifications betray the presence of BOB within Leland, as he at once tenderly cherishes and aggressively abuses his daughter; and also the phase transitions when Truddi Chase is handed over from one personality to another. Every physical comportment is the immanent product of a struggle or a pact among competing demonic forces: hence the violent, yet often surprisingly delicate, ambivalence with which the body expresses heterogeneous or conflicting intentions. There are many layers and levels of personality, but all of them are literally *superficial*: surfaces and coverings, with yet more layers underneath. No final interiority, but masks concealing and protecting other masks. Not Freud's unconscious or Lacan's big

Other, but simply other consciousnesses, other voices and forces, each struggling with, pointing to, or further possessed by, still others.

It is because thought is so efficaciously corporeal, and not representational, that a single body is forced to contain so many selves. Every manifestation of subjectivity is a physical intrusion, a consequence of trauma, a wound: "it usually manifests itself as an unusual gash on a human body—on the chest, on the hands . . . It usually keeps getting bigger until the affected person is all wound" (**DOOM PATROL**). The wound is barely noticeable at first, a microscopic gap between neurons, an infinitesimal fracture of the skin. But it grows and grows—**IT HURTS**—until it can no longer be ignored. Sensibility begins in pain. And pain forces me to think, even as it forces me to scream. An alien overfullness of sensation paralyzes the nerves, suspends the autonomic processes, hollows out a blank between action and reaction. Consciousness then arises in the depths of the violated flesh; it emerges at the very point of this cut, this intrusion. I think when, and because, I am unable to act. So long as things proceed according to habit, my actions are automatic and I have no need to become aware. But I am forced to think when I am confronted with some absurdity, some pain, when things no longer fit together on their own. Deleuze (following Bergson) and Morse Peckham (following the American pragmatists) both suggest that subjectivity is located in the gap between stimulus and response: it is the indeterminacy, the space of randomization, the temporal delay in the sensorimotor apparatus by virtue of which the latter is no longer a linear function and predictable consequence of the former. Every "self" is a singularity or a wound: a bifurcation threshold in the language of chaos theory. Selfhood is a violent rent in the fabric of my being; every quirk of my personality is a point on the catastrophe curve, the trace of a discontinuity in the course of my life.

It should come as no surprise, then, that personalities multiply under what Walter Benjamin calls the "shocks" of commodity capitalism, and that the peculiarly American affliction of Multiple Personality Disorder reached epidemic proportions at the very moment when the Republicans escalated from merely abusing their own daughters in the privacy of their own homes to systematically and publicly abusing the entire nation. For personality is the commodified product of trauma, the 'surplus value' arising from repeated exposure to shock and stress. A personality trait is not a preexisting structure or an originary essence, but always an unpredictable *alteration*, the freshly crystallized outcome of a chaotic phase transition. This is the operating principle that guides the research of Niles Caulder, the Chief of the **DOOM PATROL**, as he deliberately provokes 'accidents' that transform self-satisfied conformists into companionless, existentially tormented super-heroes. But the experimentation can work in both directions. If this is the story of your suffering, it is also the story of how you were able to survive a long history of abuse, and continue to function in the world. You found yourself repeatedly trapped in a double bind: you couldn't stand the pain, but you also couldn't do anything to abolish it. So each time you nominated a representative, a *self*, to experience the pain in your place. Blanchot writes that the "I" is left behind in moments of extremity; it cannot register the shock that pushes it or alters it beyond a certain threshold. But *somebody* is always there to witness my pain, even if "I" am not. Whatever happens to Truddi Chase, there is always *somebody* to register and respond to it: "someone within the Troop formation screamed a thought." Each new outrage on the part of the stepfather impels the traumatized body of Truddi Chase to manifest and express itself through a new personality.

Tolstoy wrote that all happy families are alike, while each unhappy family is unhappy in its own way; only he forgot to add that all families are unhappy. Truddi Chase is simply the most extreme—and therefore the most typical—example. "I feel your pain," is what Oprah so frequently says. Well, every body has at some point nominated representatives to feel its pain and to be its selves; every self is to some extent the survivor and witness of a catastrophe. Child abuse is passed like a contagion from father to daughter, from Leland to Laura. We suffer, not from *lack*, but from vertiginous epistemological overload. Each of us has endured too great a plenitude of being: too much pain, too much sensation, too much consciousness, and finally too many personalities or selves. If we're existentially incoherent, this is not because (as Freud and Lacan would have it) identity is precariously poised over an abyss, suspended on the mystery of a grand Other, or grounded in primordial absence. It is rather because we have all too much identity. Every interruption of my being introduces new forces into my body, and generates new patterns of thought and behavior. The hysterical conversion of the flesh, which Freud interpreted as a rebus of repressed reminiscences, is better understood as a literal production of fresh sensibility. The more we suffer, the more we have identity thrust upon us, even to unwanted excess. We are each distinct selves, different from one another, precisely to the extent that we are all victims of family values like togetherness, quality time, and moral training, as well as of the relentless discipline of the marketplace. The very procedures that are employed to standardize and control us in fact drive us berserk, pushing us to a point of random and unpredictable metamorphosis. Every self is a mutant or a freak. Gabba gabba, we accept you, we accept you, one of us. No wonder the bizarre, 'differently endowed' beings in Frank Henenlotter's *Basket Case 3* proudly affirm their self-esteem with a campy rendition of that old favorite song, "I've Got Personality."

So this is the history incised in your flesh, the story of "how one becomes what one is." The hardest thing to accept is that you actually got off on the abuse, that you were aroused by it, even as you felt crushed and violated. Your blood flowed, you shook with a panic attack from being trapped in the corner, your stomach felt like it was being torn apart, your bones ached from his weight, the stench of his breath made you want to retch; yet your genitals were convulsed with spasms of pleasure. That's the one thing you'll never be able to forgive. That he used you as an instrument for his own excitement is bad enough; but that he forced you to be complicit in the process is truly horrifying and unbearable. Unspeakably obscene that *jouissance* should have come from *him*. But the body has a terrifying logic of its own: "what doesn't kill me makes me stronger," as Nietzsche says. You thought that you were going to die, that it would be better to die; and instead you emerged from the torment with one personality the more. In the course of so much suffering, your sensibility was heightened and multiplied: so that you extracted—even in spite of yourself—a certain surplus value of enjoyment. This realization makes it impossible for you to play the martyr, to turn victimization into vicious self-righteousness in the manner of Andrea Dworkin. For this surplus value of enjoyment is the mark of a possession that can never be denied or exorcised: "the father in all of us" (Karen Finley), or the Republican who can never be voted out of office. And this is why the self will always remain more than one. The Troops for Truddi Chase reject the integration of the personality as a therapeutic goal, seeing it as a kind of soul murder. Better that the many learn to negotiate among themselves. For as **DOOM PATROL**'s Crazy Jane puts it, "there is no 'me.' To limit ourselves to one way of seeing and thinking would be to diminish our potential, you know? Everyone has a voice. It's like seeing the world from every angle at the same time."

15. PHILIP PULLMAN

"Oh, I'm so horny. I'm so horny all the time. You know what my Daddy said? Daddy said I was a little slut and when I grew up, I'd do it for money. And you know what? He was right. Except I don't even want money. I just want to do it." This voice belongs to Scarlet Harlot, the most flamboyant among the 64 personalities of **DOOM PATROL**'s Crazy Jane. She has only one thing in mind, and she certainly dresses the part: blonde wig, red brassiere, red miniskirt, long red gloves, stockings and garter belt, red high-heeled shoes. The cliché of raw sex, the 'essence' of femininity in drag display. Scarlet Harlot just wants to get laid, only nobody is man enough (or woman enough) to satisfy her. Her excess of orgone energy floods Happy Harbor, Rhode Island, provoking frenzied mass hallucinations and orgies in the streets, inspiring surgical operations to create new organs of pleasure, and otherwise inciting the "total eroticization of everything." But too much is never enough. Scarlet Harlot still can't get no satisfaction. She jerks off compulsively, reaching into the etheric plane and producing "ectoplasmic mannequins for her own shameless gratification."

And she consumes these sex toys, one after another. Disarticulated dummy parts lie strewn across her bedroom. So many warn out phallic appendages, heaps of grotesque prosthetic arms, legs, heads. Did you know that materialized ectoplasm looks a lot like cheap plastic?

Our postmodern myths are all modular, standardized, prosthetic constructions: Barbie and Ken dolls, or department store dummies with interchangeable parts. "Blue eyes, blonde hair, tight body, long legs, she's glamorous, she's welcomed by boys, I wanna be Twist Barbie" (Shonen Knife). This suburban white American Barbie is the model of what every girl wishes to be (even if, like the members of Shonen Knife, she is neither white nor American). Todd Haynes, in his banned film *Superstar*, presents Karen Carpenter as literally a Barbie doll. For isn't such an image the real basis, or inner secret, of Karen's saintliness and suffering? No human female could physically endure actual embodiment in Barbie's ultra-slim proportions. Her bones would be too thin and brittle, the force of gravity too strong. Not to mention the unbearable agony of elongating, emaciating, and eviscerating your flesh. Strange *jouissance*, restricting yourself to a diet of salads and ice tea, emptying out your intestinal tract with Ex-Lax and Ipecac. The anorexic Passion of Karen Carpenter lies in the ecstasy and terror of this evacuation, the unendurable stresses of her new incarnation in vinyl and plastic. Corporeality is vomited out, or transposed into song. Flesh and voice alike are stretched to the limit, stereotypically processed and purified, captured and commodified at the most excruciating vanishing point. Parents and brother, record producers and music critics, President Nixon and the medical establishment and suburban real estate developers and multinational corporations: they all conspired to teach Karen Carpenter how to be a woman, to imprison her, skin, bones, organs, and breath, in an idealized, prosthetic self.

Scarlet Harlot and Karen Carpenter: sex and anti-sex, whore and virgin, the two poles of the feminine mystique. Femininity is a stereotype, not an archetype. Madonna and Cindy Sherman understand this; Camille Paglia doesn't have a clue. It's just like using makeup: you've got to "put on a happy face," or at the very least 'put on your face' each morning in front of the mirror. "Faces are not basically individual . . . You don't so much have a face, as slide into one . . . It is faces that choose their subjects," and not the reverse (Deleuze and Guattari). Along similar lines, Allucquere Roseanne Stone tells us that in virtual reality research "there is talk of renting prepackaged body forms complete with voice and touch . . . multiple personality as commodity fetish!" In cyberspace, nobody can hear you scream. But the bathroom mirror is already a kind of cyberspace, already a virtual reality. As you stare at that image in the mirror, you discover that the face staring back at you was already there long before you, just waiting for you to assume it. Good little girls must be seen and not heard; they have to look just so. Bad girls are just asking for it, you can tell by the way they dress. In either case, the image precedes the object, the reflection always has to come first. That's why you must spend hours in front of the mirror, agonizing over the right outfit for tonight's date. Crazy Jane is a slut because that's what Daddy told her to be. Karen Carpenter is a goody-two-shoes because that's the image her managers established for her, and her fans came to expect. When I change clothes or put on makeup or rub gel into my hair, I'm only trying to compose my face, the better to conform to my reflection. Deleuze and Guattari write of the inhuman *horror* of the standard white Euro-American face, Jesus face or Barbie face: "a lunar landscape, with its pores, planes, matts, bright colors, whiteness, and holes." The stereotype existed before me, I was born to embody it.

People in primitive societies flay the skin of their enemies, thereby depriving them of their souls. But we in postmodern America prefer to discipline the body by adding ever more epidermal layers, multiplying faces, images, and souls. In the power relations that define our society, "the soul is the prison of the body," and not the reverse (Foucault). And thus we imprison our own bodies, as well as those of others. It's all done with mirrors. Even the psychopathic killer Buffalo Bill, in *The Silence of the Lambs*, only strips the flesh off his victims in order thence to sew a second skin for himself. It's just like when you go under the knife for a breast implant or a nose job. From applied cosmetology to tattooing to plastic and prosthetic surgery, our postmodern culture has developed a whole art of distending and adorning the skin. The face is less a mask or a disguise, Deleuze and Guattari suggest, than it is the mark of an evacuation of the depths, a libidinous transformation of the entire body into surface, and nothing but surface. Ex-Lax and Ipecac of the soul. Philip Pullman, in his fine novel *Galatea*, imagines a future in which, thanks to the visionary interventions of multinational capital, "nothing was immutable, everything was subject to change, including the most private and secret regions of the soul . . . The outward appearance of people could change, and so could their natures. Businessmen could become musicians, musicians become businessmen, thus illustrating the multiplicity of phenomena and the unity of matter." In postmodern epidermal space, "nothing is hidden," as Wittgenstein rightly insists: "since everything lies open to view there is nothing to explain." Love means never having to say you're sorry.

One summer I bleached my hair and colored it purple. I sat in that chair in the beauty salon for four hours. The plaster I applied to the surface of my scalp adhered to my skin, burned painfully into my flesh, clung to me so tightly that I couldn't get it off. Afterwards, I was strangely captivated by the new self that stared at me from out of the mirror. Who was I, what had I become? Never underestimate the adhesive power of appearances. Such cosmetic and prosthetic transformations are all perfectly real. Adorning the skin, acquiring a face, is an actual process of physical transformation. Karen Carpenter lived and died for this. It is also what seals the fate of Mr. Nobody, the Dadaist politician and psychedelic prankster of **DOOM PATROL**. Mr. Nobody is "the abstract man, the virtual man, the notional man," literally a man without a face. He is drawn as a sort of sketchy, two-dimensional Synthetic Cubist assemblage, all sharp disjunctive rectangles with lots of interstitial space. Freed from the burden of identity, as a result of being subjected to bizarre sensory-deprivation experiments, Mr. Nobody is able to be nowhere and everywhere at once. He transforms Paris into a virtual-reality art playground, and provokes an epidemic of LSD hallucinations across the USA. He even runs for President, outdoing Ross Perot as a lightning rod for voter discontent. Mr. Nobody's surreal, modernist abstraction opens a space of limitless metamorphosis.

But such things mustn't be allowed to happen here; this is America, after all. Even a superhero must be confined to a 'secret identity.' And so Mr. Nobody meets his antitype: John "Yankee Doodle" Dandy, an old comic book character who is faceless because he has too many identities, instead of too few. Dandy has been driven insane by his ability to simulate any and every personality. Metamorphically fluid, he is scarcely more reliable or more patriotic than Mr. Nobody; if the Pentagon is able to appropriate Dandy as a secret weapon, it's only because "you point him in the right direction and hope to God that when the shit stops flying, the enemy is in worse shape than you are." Dandy's own visage is blank and robotic, with ever-changing Scrabble tiles for eyes. But a ring of stereotypical faces floats in the air above him, like balls for him to juggle, or like a sinister wreath or halo: "the faces howl, like dogs, harried by thoughts . . . faces buzzing like bees, hungry and thirsty." Indeed, nothing is more horrible than the cruel rapacity of a human face. And so John Dandy destroys Mr. Nobody by literally thrusting one of these faces upon him, imprisoning him in a visage of banality and boredom. "I am somebody" is the great, deluded American rallying cry. Mr. Nobody is turned into somebody—and thus brought back to order and reason—when he is given a determinate face, trapped in a fixed expression that clings to him like a leech. "It's such a gamble when you get a face" (Richard Hell). Whoever can be recognized can be made accountable, held responsible, regimented, punished, and finally killed. They give you a face so they can take an ID photo. Identity is a straightjacket that you can't ever remove.

But even if you can't escape, you can always hope to change one look for another. It isn't a question of truth, but one of simulation. The point is not to 'save the appearances,' but to heighten and improve them. The very same mechanisms that were invented to make me responsible, to chain me to myself, also open the doors to frivolity, irresponsibility, and a sort of divine innocence. Nietzsche vastly prefers aestheticians to moralists and metaphysicians, because the former are blithely unconcerned with 'high seriousness,' with otherworldly heights and depths, or with inner essences. Artists and cosmeticians are the last people who would ever bother to hearken patiently to the voice of Being. Rather they give us back the world again, as appearance and nothing but appearance: "for 'appearance' here signifies reality *once more*," Nietzsche says, "only selected, strengthened, corrected." The truest facial expression is the most insincere, stereotypical and superficial. And that's why appearances are never deceiving. "Everything is what it seems," says the epigraph to *Galatea*. Clothes make the man, or the woman, as all drag queens and fashion models know. You create yourself anew each morning, every time you get dressed, every time your body adopts particular postures and gestures, every time your face fixes itself in certain expressions. With the right clothes and makeup and hairdo, you can choose any identity, embody any fantasy, transform yourself into anything you want to be. Each year Madonna comes forth with a new likeness, a new wardrobe, a whole new borrowed personality. That's the American way. The glamorous images of your desire are always already there, available for instant purchase: they are recycled from some old film, and draped on a mannequin in a window at Bloomingdale's or Nordstrom's. You can become whatever you pay for—and easy credit terms can always be arranged. So let us not be bothered that our faces are never our own, that our actions and reactions are pre-programmed, or that our most private feelings and most intimate moments involve repertoires of behavior that we've picked up by imitating others. Just ride the waves of fashion. As neuroscientists Ronald Melzack and Patrick Wall have recently shown, even the inner experience of pain is "largely the result of learned behavior." We capitalize on stereotypes. No gain, no pain. But that doesn't make the headache I am feeling now any less intense, or any less real; I've learned my childhood lessons far too well.

Art and capitalism alike are tirelessly engaged in the great project of selecting and refining appearances, stimulating monstrous and artificial desires, improving the tone of the skin. *Galatea* is filled with delirious visions of new capital investment: strange mechanical devices, enormous and splendidly glittering cities, vast factories hidden in Third World jungles whose assembly lines mass-produce beautiful, gracious robots. Martin Browning, the narrator of *Galatea*, transforms himself from an impoverished musician into a millionaire entrepreneur, after undergoing a long apprenticeship in appearances. He is seduced and initiated into the art of living vicariously, by procuration or by pretense. Money changes everything. And "change happens when one state imitates another one, because it desires it." You can always find a face that suits your needs of the moment. If you don't know anything about art, for instance, you (or your corporation) can hire somebody who does. Love follows the same pattern. Martin's true beloved, the eponymous heroine of *Galatea*, is described as an angel, an idealized, otherworldly being, a male fantasy of absolute, pristine beauty—which means, as Martin finally discovers, that "she" is a hermaphroditic automaton manufactured in the factories of the Perfect City. But it's of no consequence to Martin's desire whether Galatea is made of flesh and blood, or of wires and microchips; nor whether Galatea has "a boy's sex, or a girl's, or some inconceivable both, or [whether she is] blank and smooth like a statue" (indeed, though Galatea is referred to throughout with feminine pronouns, her anatomical gender remains a mystery for most of the novel; Martin only fucks her in the ass, and from behind, so that he never gets a chance to see or touch her pubic regions). For desire is a matter, not of "lack," but of prosthesis, of pure pretense. Its objects are neither missing nor lost, but exquisitely artificial; that is, as Deleuze and Guattari say, they simply need to be produced. The real is entirely prefabricated, and whatever has been fabricated is thereby perfectly real: "nothing is natural any more, and nothing is artificial," says Martin towards the end of *Galatea*. "It's a false dichotomy, and we should forget about it. We all show false faces to the world, and a good thing too, for a hundred reasons."

So long live the false face—or lots of them, the more the merrier. If we can't escape recognition altogether—witness the fate of Mr. Nobody—we may as well enhance our visibility, court recognition with a vengeance. Incarnate ourselves as talking heads. All we need is media access, and a sufficient line of credit. When I was in high school, I told my guidance counselor that my career goal was to become a celebrity game show panelist. Or at least a contestant on *The Gong Show*. Better to be gonged by Jaye P. Morgan, than not to appear on TV at all. To be truly faceless—without a reflection, like a vampire—is to be deprived of being, to be cut adrift without the requisite purchasing power, an orphan of the night, a lost soul. No face without a Visa card, no Visa card without a face. Martin Browning encounters such lost souls: the Unreal People, light as feathers, insubstantial as ghosts. You can't look at the Unreal People directly, but only from the corner of your eye. As they have little power to affect you, you can't keep them steadily in mind and you tend even to forget that they are there. People become Unreal when their lines of credit are exhausted, and when their savings have dwindled as a result of inflation. They get ever thinner and more transparent, as they become progressively unable to acquire new identities, unable to shop, purchase, and consume. They've gone through the cycle, and reached the last extremity, of what my old elementary school textbook defined as the "four freedoms" of capitalism: "freedom to try, freedom to buy, freedom to sell, freedom to fail."

The Unreals cling to this fourth and final "freedom," having exhausted the previous three. Their residual subsistence certainly cannot be regarded as a condition of deprivation or lack. Think of it rather as an *effect*—an entirely positive expression—of the harsh pressures of the marketplace, or the rigors of natural selection. Inflation is a constant environmental hazard, the sinister flip side of capital accumulation. But inflation is only possible in the first place because the will to simulate and to expend is universal. Marx with his theories of commodity fetishism never went far enough. *Galatea* has a much more radical vision: it proposes that money is the vitalistic principle animating matter, the *élan vital* of all living

and desirous beings. Money is inherently voluptuous and promiscuous; it tends to multiply at a geometric rate if unchecked by
Malthusian constraints. The contagious "germ" of inflation, once
it is introduced into an economy, rages to epidemic proportions.
Cutthroat competition in capitalism or in nature, the notorious
'survival of the fittest,' is only the counter-effect of an outrageous
original exuberance; for "the general aspect of life is not hunger
and distress, but rather wealth, luxury, even absurd prodigality"
(Nietzsche, commenting on Darwin). *Galatea* similarly teaches a
delirious lesson of infinite simulation, infinite libido, and infinite
credit: "Electricity! Money! Love! Happiness! Matter loving itself,
making love to itself, that's what it all is ... Electricity, and
finance, and sexuality, and happiness, and evolution, they all come
about because of the amorous inclinations of matter."

Let us then pursue these amorous inclinations on our own
accounts. Pretend beyond all measure, and send the orgone levels
soaring. Follow the lead of Crazy Jane as Scarlet Harlot: reinvent
sexual promiscuity and rapaciousness with the aid of prosthetic
stimulants. Let simulated masculinity and femininity run amok. As
Kathy Acker says in a recent interview, apropos of vibrators and
dildoes: "packing is gonna make a major revolution! And the only
thing guys have to learn is that there's nothing wrong with dicks
and cocks, but don't think you've got the only cocks in the world."
Severo Sarduy correspondingly writes that the aim of the drag
queen is "to be more and more of a woman, until the line is crossed
and woman is surpassed; transvestites, like insects, are *hypertelic*:
they pass beyond their goals." Such extravagance and gratuitous
display is the most urgent tendency of late capitalist culture, even
as it is of arms races and sexual selection in biological evolution.
Stereotype is transformed into singularity, and habit is heightened
into intensity, not when these oppressive steady states are furiously
negated, but rather when they are embraced with a cool, measured
enthusiasm, carefully refined and stylized, pushed just a little too
far. Such is the credo, if not quite of Mr. Nobody, then of another
of Grant Morrison's creations, Sebastian O. Sebastian lives in an
alternate Victorian world—a 'steampunk' world—one which has

computers and video. He's the virtual-reality equivalent of Oscar Wilde: an aesthete and dandy who's all too pleased to live in a universe of artifice and simulation. "It is our duty to be as artificial as possible," he proclaims. "One must commit acts of the highest treason only when dressed in the most resplendent finery."

16. ANDY WARHOL

To be obsessed with images, with surfaces, with appearances: what does it really mean? In particular, what did it mean to Andy Warhol? Images are nothing like objects. When things retreat into their images, the way they do on TV, they lose their solidity, their palpability, their presence. Images have a weightlessness that is both mysterious and soothing. They haunt us, like ghosts; they empty out space, the better to flicker interminably in the void. Images are premised upon a visibility so extreme that it relegates the world to a state of almost transparency. They resemble their objects so utterly, so perfectly, that the objects themselves become almost invisible. The most perfect resemblance, Maurice Blanchot says, is the one that has "no name and no face." An artist is somebody who wants to turn the whole world into images; but he usually ends up making more objects instead. That is at least how Warhol regards the matter: "I really believe in empty spaces," he says; "although, as an artist, I make a lot of junk . . . I can't even empty my own spaces." It's a dilemma that assaults him day after day: "I'm sure I'm going to look in the mirror and see no one, nothing. People are always calling me a mirror and if a mirror looks into a mirror, what is there to see?" Maybe that would even be the most satisfying outcome. If only Andy could vanish into the mirror, into the camera, into the tape recorder... To be an empty image, and nothing but an image, just like Marilyn or James Dean or Elvis... But try as Andy may, his body never entirely disappears. Instead, "day after day I look in the mirror and I still see something—a new pimple. If the pimple on my upper right cheek is gone, a new one turns up on my lower left cheek, on my jawline, near my ear, in the middle of my nose, under the hair on my eyebrows, right between my eyes. I think it's the same pimple, moving from place to place." This pimple, you might say, is Warhol's fleshly double, his abject objecthood, the thing that binds him to his body, or to himself. The thing that prevents him from turning into an image. "Nudity," Warhol tells us, "is a threat to my existence"; and the pimple is the point where he's exposed naked, for all the world to see. Your blemishes are the most intimate secrets you have; but they are also the first things that everyone else notices. That's why Warhol "believe[s] in low lights and trick mirrors . . . [and] in plastic surgery." You can never have too many skin creams and lotions and ointments.

No moral, aesthetic, or metaphysical issue is more important for Warhol than the question of how to get rid of pimples. "If someone asked me, 'What's your problem?'", he tells us, "I'd have to say, 'Skin.'" And he's right, of course. Everything that matters is already out there, right on the surface. "Don't think, but look!" as Wittgenstein said. Faced with the trauma of an acne outburst, or with the heartbreak of psoriasis, I must learn not to bother with searching out deep structures and root causes. For such disorders can only be treated topically and symptomatically: that is to say, only on the level of surfaces and effects. It's impossible to dig down to the origin; the best solutions for skin problems are always aesthetic or cosmetic ones. As my trusty old *Home Medical Guide* puts it: "Since the cause of acne is frequently misunderstood, the 'victim' may be accused of being responsible for his or her condition. Parents often blame their youngsters for eating too much junk food, eating too little, eating too much, not washing properly, not getting enough sleep, sleeping too much, being obsessed with the opposite sex, having no interest in the opposite sex, ad infinitum. The truth is, none of these things has anything to do with acne, and if there is any 'blame' attached to the disorder, it may well belong to the parents' genes . . . No exact cause is known." Parents are all too likely to read acne as a sign of deviance: of not being properly heterosexual, most likely. But a careful, patient attention to images and surfaces undoes all such imputations of guilt. As Nietzsche says in a similar context, "that no one is any longer made accountable . . . *this alone is the great liberation*—thus alone is the *innocence* of becoming restored." Warhol scrupulously abstains from pejorative judgments: "It's so nice, whatever it is. I approve of what everybody does: it must be right because somebody said it was right. I wouldn't judge anybody." Instead, he dispenses expert advice on skin care: "I dunk a Johnson and Johnson cotton ball into Johnson and Johnson rubbing alcohol and rub the cotton ball against the pimple." Or again: "if you have a pimple, put on the pimple cream in a way that will make it really stand out." Or yet again: "Haven't you heard about those ladies who take young guys to the theater and jerk them off so that they can put it all over their face? . . . It sort of pulls it tighter and makes them younger for the evening." If one remedy doesn't work, then simply try another. In the end, Warhol says, "I've never met a person I couldn't call a beauty. Each person has beauty at some point in their lifetime."

Warhol, too, shows us how to "have done with the judgment of God"; but in a far gentler manner than Nietzsche or Artaud. I suppose that's why it's no big deal that he went to church every Sunday. For Warhol has none of the anxieties that plagued his great Modernist forbears, none of their transgressive urges or buried *ressentiment*. Why worry, if nothing is true, and everything is permitted? Lacan says somewhere that the real formula of atheism is not, 'God is dead,' but rather, 'God is unconscious.' If that is so, then Warhol—whatever his private observances—was undoubtedly the least pious of men. When everything's just an image, there's no

Symbolic Order left to transgress. And that goes not only for God, but for all the other fetishes of modernist faith as well: sex, money, and politics. They all come down to appearances, and nothing but appearances. Sometimes a penis is just a penis, is what Freud ought to have said. Think of it not as the Phallus, but as a convenient dispenser of facial cream. Castration is a matter merely of local and passing significance. The organ is nothing in itself; it's all a question of how you use it. And there are as many different uses as there are different male and female bodies. "Everybody has a different idea of love," Warhol writes. "One girl I know said, 'I knew he loved me when he didn't come in my mouth.'"

That's what Warhol's religion really comes down to. "The Factory was a church," Gary Indiana writes, "the Church of the Unimaginable Penis, or something . . . The sanctity of the institution and its rituals is what's important, not personal salvation. Maintaining the eternal surface." Maintaining the image, you might say. Nothing is hidden in Andy's church, and nothing is transcendent: what you see is exactly what you get. Movie and media stars are the only objects of worship. Only Elvis or James Dean can tell me what it is to be a man. Or some other icon of the time: maybe, even, Fidel Castro. Castro was a hot media figure in the 60s, though his glamour has faded considerably since then. It's odd, the way his name always used to come up. At one point in Warhol's 1967 film *Nude Restaurant*, Taylor Mead teasingly claims, in close-up straight to the camera, that "I was in Fidel Castro's dictionary . . . I made it with the Big One, Big Number One of Cuba." Viva responds by telling how, in pre-Revolutionary Cuba, a political prisoner was castrated by Batista's secret police for refusing to talk. At which Mead muses, in that offhand, campy manner of his: "you would think Castro would be the castrator." In fact, several years before this film was made the CIA had indeed plotted, if not to castrate Castro outright, at least to devirilize him by lacing his food with female sex hormones. They figured that his beard would fall out, and his voice become high-pitched and squeaky. Once Castro's macho image was ruined, they thought, he could easily be overthrown. An obsession with Fidel's sexuality seems to be present in other CIA projects of the time as well, such as the plan to kill him with an exploding cigar. This may well be one of those times when a cigar isn't just a cigar. Isn't the United States government's hysteria about the Castro regime—one that still persists today, even after 36 years—the result of envy and fear at the prospect of Fidel's "Big One"? The CIA spooks never succeeded in putting any of their strange schemes into action; but the very existence of such plans testifies to the potency, as it were, of Fidel's media image. Just like a pimple that won't go away, his flashy and fleshly presence on the international scene in the early 60s was an affront to *norteamericano* manliness as then embodied by John F. Kennedy. Following the Kennedy assassination, Lyndon Johnson more prudently (if no more successfully) decided to pick on Ho Chi Minh instead. After all, nobody would exactly say that old Uncle Ho had sex appeal.

Warhol, for his part, goes JFK and the CIA one better when it comes to devirilizing Castro. In his 1965 film *The Life of Juanita Castro*, not only does Fidel's estranged, anti-communist sister take center stage, but Fidel, his brother Raul, and Che Guevara are all played by women. This gender reversal testifies to the fluidity of postmodern bodies. It's not really a matter of deflating Castro's ego, or his cock, but of showing how his potency—how virility in general—is always an affair of bluff and display, of pure pretense. That's just show business. In the world of Warhol's Factory, castrator and castrated, or Castro and castration, are able to exchange places with the utmost of ease. Warhol describes the idea of the film as "fags on the sugar plantation"; he renders the Cuban Revolution as high camp. In Marxist terms, history is repeated a second time, as farce. Warhol's treatment not only outdoes the CIA, but trumps Hollywood as well: it is even more campy and over-the-top than Richard Fleischer's 1969 would-be blockbuster *Che!*, despite the latter's amazing casting of Omar Sharif as Guevara and Jack Palance as Fidel. *The Life of Juanita Castro* is ostensibly based on a *Life* magazine article in which Juanita denounces her brother as a tyrant. But it is actually inspired, Warhol claims, by reports that Raul Castro was a transvestite, and that Fidel himself had made "attempts to become a Hollywood star," and had even appeared as an extra in an Esther Williams musical. Was the Cuban revolutionary regime's notorious persecution of gay men a result of Castro's own sense of masculine panic, his need to bury a disreputable past? Warhol's film, you might say, presents a new Fidel, releasing his bitchy inner queen from the prison of Marxist-Leninist virility. The romantic machismo of Third World revolution runs a poor second to the sexually more ambiguous allure of celluloid stardom.

The Life of Juanita Castro is a wonderfully *skewed* film, in all sorts of ways. The actors sit in rows, facing the place of the camera, with Juanita front center and Fidel and Che on either side of her. Except that the supposed camera to which the actors always direct themselves is not the one that actually shoots the film. We see the stage instead from an oblique angle, well off to the right. The result is that, for instance, when Juanita or Fidel 'steps up to the camera' for a monologue and a close-up, she actually moves out of frame. The show must go on, but it isn't really being addressed to us: for we are way too off-center to engage it. This formal absurdity is only heightened by how the script is presented to us. Ronald Tavel, Warhol's screenwriter, sits on stage along with the rest of the cast. He reads aloud from his script, telling the actors what to do and say. "Fidel, smoke your cigar for a while with great satisfaction." "Juanita, say to Fidel, 'You never really cared about the poor peasants.'" "Fidel, turn to Juanita and yell, 'Puta! Gusana!'" The actor then repeats the line or follows the instruction, usually with over-emphatic gestures and intonations, but trying—with more or less success—to keep a straight face during the process. Marie Menken, who plays Juanita, has an especially hard time. She seems fairly sloshed throughout the film, frequently mumbling or mispronouncing lines, totally garbling Spanish phrases, and querulously complaining that the words she's been told to recite don't make any sense. Sitting in a wicker chair, fanning herself, and taking occasional swigs of beer, she displays all the mannerisms of a fallen *grande dame*. Overall, she exudes an air of amused indifference mingled with haughty disdain, as if to say, 'I can't believe I'm doing this.' Menken's 'bad' performance is the most memorable thing about the film, but all the actors have their moments. At times, Tavel instructs the entire cast to laugh, or cry, or smile as if for a family portrait. The result is something like a well-orchestrated political rally: the same stereotypical actions and expressions are manifested at once by everybody present. The whole film, in effect, is being dictated as we watch: which is just right for a film about a dictator. Language, as Deleuze and Guattari put it, is a performance and not a structure: "the transmission of the word as order-word, not the communication of a sign as information." *The Life of Juanita Castro* thus *performs* the Cuban Revolution as camp spectacle, rather than *informing* us of its accomplishments or failures. Which is why Warhol says, deadpan, that the political "point" of the film is, "it depends on how you want to look at it."

Nothing could be further from the old familiar practices of ideology-critique and the alienation-effect. We aren't deceived or stupefied by this spectacle; but it doesn't give us space for critical reflection either. This is a point that Warhol's critics have often misunderstood. We're usually asked to choose between two readings of Warhol's work: one that praises him for exposing the institutional structures of commodity capitalism and the art world, and one that condemns him for being in complicity with these same institutional structures. But aren't both of these readings beside the point? After all, "if a mirror looks into a mirror, what is there to see?" Of course Warhol is in complicity, and of course he is always calling attention to that complicity. But the real interest of his work lies elsewhere. It's too late: the political and art worlds are high camp already. You may hate "the society of the spectacle" with a puritanical fervor, as the Castro regime so ostentatiously does, or as Guy Debord and the Situationists did. But if you care at all for pleasure, if the old corrupt Yankee-controlled Havana of nightclubs, casinos, and whorehouses holds any allure for you whatsoever, then such purism and puritanism clearly won't do. You'll have to work around and within the spectacle, just as Andy did. Near the end of *Juanita Castro*, Fidel accuses Juanita of opposing his regime only for the sake of publicity, just in order to further her career as a singer and dancer. "But I am a great singer, I am a great dancer," Juanita scornfully replies.

Isn't that the point, right there in a nutshell? As Nietzsche said, even philosophers ought to learn how to dance. What good is virile self-control, or political and aesthetic discipline, compared to the pleasures of a good Cuban cigar and (with a nod to Che) of an Argentinian tango? Warhol recounts asking Emile de Antonio, in the late 50s, why he was having trouble finding acceptance in the art world. "You're too swish," de Antonio replied; "you play up the swish—it's like an armor with you." And, Warhol adds, "it was all too true . . . I certainly wasn't a butch kind of guy by nature, but I must admit, I went out of my way to play up the other extreme." Come the 60s, this strategy finally paid off. I distrust any account of Warhol, no matter how celebratory, that doesn't take his swishiness into account. If nothing else, Warhol says, he "always had a lot of fun with [the 'swish' thing]—just watching the expressions on people's faces." Of course, this sort of campy aestheticism has been a common strategy of survival for gay men for quite a long time: at least since the invention of hetero- and homosexuality in the later 19th century. Oscar Wilde, Jean Genet, and Michel Foucault all urge us to transform ourselves into works of art. If Warhol is "the last dandy," as Stephen Koch calls him, it's because he pushes this posture further than anyone else. Warhol is the first to understand that the whole postmodern world is in drag, and not just certain special individuals. In Marxist terms, the actual conditions of production have already outrun whatever we may think and say about them. Warhol is content merely to dramatize this fact. There's no place for us to look, except into the mirror. There's nothing left to do, except go to another party. There are no real men and no real women; it's all insinuation. "I dreamed of scented rooms and endless permutations of identity: boys becoming girls, girls becoming boys who do boys like they're girls," as Grant Morrison writes in his recent comic, *The Invisibles*. Despite Warhol's massive postmortem institutionalization, his swishy aesthetic retains its provocative force today. It's a permanent reproach to the American cult of virility. It's scarcely possible to take seriously any more, after Warhol, all those tough, high-minded claims these days for an art of political critique on the one hand, and for an art that teaches virtue on the other.

And that's the difference between Warhol and the CIA. The CIA sought in all seriousness to subvert Castro: to castrate him literally or metaphorically, to subject him to the Law of the Father. To render him accountable, in one way or another. Warhol, in contrast, frivolously seeks to *pervert* Castro: to dress him in drag, and perhaps to drag him into bed. That's what drives the gender play in *The Life of Juanita Castro*. Behind every great man stands a woman, popular wisdom says; and in this case, Fidel himself is also that woman. Mercedes Ospina plays a rather butch Fidel, swaggering and smirking her way through the part. But she isn't in drag; she makes no attempt to pass for a man. She's just there, in a dress and without a beard. For masculinity is an image and not an object: a superficial performance, rather than an attribute of bodies. It's Fidel's very womanliness that drives him to act so butch. The effect of Ospina's performance is that of an infinite hall of mirrors: a woman playing a man who is really a woman in the guise of a man. Tavel's script heightens the atmosphere of silly delirium. It gleefully mixes political clichés, bitchy reproaches and insults, and moments of absurd overdramatization. At one point, Fidel makes an excruciatingly long speech in bad Spanish (it consumes a full 15 minutes of screen time), while the other actors all fall asleep and snore loudly. (Castro, of course, is as notorious for his long speeches as Warhol is for seemingly interminable films like *Sleep* and *Empire*). The film also abounds in sly sexual innuendoes, and in teasing flirtations between the various players: especially between those two big *maricones*, Raul and Che. It's much more fun to casually cruise a Party meeting than to work twelve hours straight in the hot sun cutting sugar cane. Politics is pervaded and perverted by desire: not by that big, fatal passion that consumes your very being, but by those silly little whims and compulsions that vex you from day to day. Marxism and masculinity must both be redefined. Fidel Castro is nothing but a capricious, bitchy diva, spoiled rotten by too much early success on the world-historical stage. His revolutionary virility is a grand production number; if he carries it off well enough, he hopes, history will absolve him. Fidel is best understood, then, as a fabulous camp icon: a dialectical Bette Davis or a Commie Joan Crawford. And now, in the late 90s, when he's become passé, still holding the line for an obsolete vision of Leninist virtue, doesn't he bear a striking resemblance to Gloria Swanson in Sunset Boulevard?

It all comes down to images, and nothing but images. Warhol's art really is about fashion and style. It couldn't care less about what's beneath the surface. Nothing could be more "corny," Warhol says, than "agonized, anguished art" that seeks to uncover hidden depths. The critical spirit finds the world to be radically deficient. Images never satisfy it; it always wants something more. But Warhol just shrugs his shoulders, and suggests that enough is enough. The world, for him, is not deficient, but, if anything, overly full. The junk we collect, Warhol warns us, will fill up all our spaces. The junk Warhol himself collected still hasn't even been catalogued properly. You may remove a pimple today, but you'll discover a new one tomorrow. There's too much out there already; why get excited about one organ more or less? The virile fear of castration is utterly foreign to Warhol. Straight men tend to get all touchy and anxious about their potency. But the straight man is only there to feed the comedian his lines. It's the latter who gets the laughter, and the money, and the applause. That's why Warhol prefers style over substance, swish over machismo, images over things. Why ever bother to dig beneath the surface? You can always make selections and corrections on the skin itself. You can add additional layers, covering acne with makeup, or treating it with sperm or with benzoyl peroxide. "When I did my self-portrait," Warhol tells us, "I left all the pimples out because you always should. Pimples are a temporary condition and they don't have anything to do with what you really look like. Always omit the blemishes—they're not part of the good picture you want."

17. DEAN MARTIN

How we love to recycle and replay the Fifties—even those of us who weren't around then. Fifties fashions, Fifties hairstyles, Fifties cars and motorcycles, Fifties music, Fifties personalities: these still define what we mean by cool. Think of James Dean, think of Marilyn, think of Elvis. Elvis, especially, eternally returns to haunt us: he's forever at the center of the American psyche. More people have encountered him dead than ever saw him when he was alive. Rumors abound: of assassination plots, faked death certificates, secret cloning programs, reincarnations, preternatural singing from closets and bathrooms, sightings on UFOs. It's all gotten so baroque, multilayered and self-referential. Even the Elvis impersonators have their own impersonators now. After all, wasn't Elvis, in the latter part of his career, when he performed in Vegas wearing that rhinestone-studded white jumpsuit, already a simulacrum of himself? Daniel Clowes, in his comic book *Eightball*, envisions a time, in the not-too-distant future, when "there will be nostalgia for the nostalgia of previous generations: 'I'm not into The Fifties per se; I'm into the Fifties revival of the Seventies!'—'Bah! I'm into more of an Eighties Fifties!'" The Fifties are the fulfillment of the American prophecy: the age, not of Aquarius, but of the Emersonian self-made man, and of Zarathustra's Eternal Return. Now, as the millennium approaches, our culture is deliriously awash in clones and replicas of the Fifties, citations and allusions, everything always carefully encased "in quotation marks." Maybe we aren't into Elvis per se, so much as we're into the idea of "being into Elvis." Elvis is rather like the mythical phallus of psychoanalysis: there but not there, a simulacral shimmering, present precisely in his absence. Sometimes we want to *have* Elvis, and sometimes we want to *be* him: but in either case we fail, since he remains a virtual image, visible but intangible, always ever so slightly beyond our reach. Elvis's talent, beauty, and grace—the sound of his voice, the ease of his smile, the swaying of his hips— are things you and I can only dream of.

Or maybe catch them at the movies. Clarence (Christian Slater), the hero of the recent film *True Romance* (written by Quentin Tarantino, and directed by Tony Scott), sways between fantasies of being Elvis, and of having him. He learns lessons of daring, courage, and devotion to his true love from conversations with Elvis in the bathroom. He marches in there to piss like a man, and there's the King staring back at him from the mirror, giving him words of encouragement and big-brotherly advice and approval: "Clarence, I've always liked you." If this carries a charge of homoerotic attachment, well then, so much the better. After all, Clarence's standard pick-up line is to tell a woman that he's not a fag or anything, but still he wouldn't mind going to bed with Elvis. That's how cool Elvis is. That tells you just how much Clarence adores the King. Wanting to sleep with Elvis is in fact the American dream: it's precisely what Clarence and the women he meets have in common. And so all the rituals of traditional male bonding and rivalry—locker room pranks, pissing contests, comparisons of penis size—get turned into something goofier and finer. The toilet, rather than Robert Bly's backwoods, is the site of Clarence's initiation into manhood. Under Elvis's benign guidance, he's transformed from a lonely nerd, who works in a comic-book store and obsessively watches martial-arts movies, into the real-life hero of his own true romance. He runs off with his girlfriend Alabama (Patricia Arquette), survives confrontations with Hollywood and the Mob, and finds health, wealth, and happiness in a nuclear family of his own, ending up on a sunny beach not far from the site of Elvis's 1963 movie masterpiece, *Fun in Acapulco*.

Elvis, now and forever, is totally cool—as the protagonists of *True Romance* never tire of reminding us. It's not so much what Elvis *means* that is important, as the sheer fact of his ubiquity. What has he done to multiply himself—even and especially after his death? Just how many of him are there? These are questions, not for hermeneutics or semiotics, but rather for population genetics. Like rabbits released in virgin territory, Elvis replicas and Elvis impersonators have wreaked havoc on our cultural ecology, overrunning and overturning the entire postmodern landscape. As soon as Elvis appeared, all the earlier crooners were driven quickly to near-extinction. Good-bye Perry Como, good-bye Bing, good-bye Frank. And no one subsequently has really been able to compete: not Mick, not Michael Jackson, not even Axl Rose or Eddie Vedder. I mean, would you trust one of *them* to be your bathroom confidant? As any evolutionary theorist will tell you, adaptive fitness is defined, not in terms of quality of life or innate value or even personal longevity, but solely in terms of ultimate reproductive success. Horrifying, but true. The body of the man, Elvis Aron Presley, was only a vehicle for that berserk replicator, the Elvis meme. And it's of no concern to the meme that the later recordings are boring, or that Elvis himself put on too much weight in those final years, and led such a lonely, empty, unfulfilled life. Andy Warhol once said that "Picasso was the artist I admired most in all of history, because he was so prolific." The greatest artist, in Warhol's view, is the one who has left the largest sheer quantity of images and copies behind. Picasso, of course, was a master in this respect: he went so far as to doodle on the backs of checks, hoping that this would induce the recipients to never cash them. But even Picasso couldn't impose his replicas upon our culture to anywhere near the extent that Elvis did. Warhol understood this perfectly:

that's why he never bothered with painting mock Picassos, as so many lesser artists have inadvertently done, but went right ahead and silkscreened multiples of the King.

Of all the crooners of that era, none has vanished so utterly and so precipitously as Dean Martin. Throughout the Fifties, and all the way into the late Sixties, his singles and albums reached the Billboard Top Forty, his TV specials were close to the top in the Nielsens, his nightclub act was the biggest draw in Vegas, and his movies were huge blockbuster hits. And then, all of a sudden, nothing. Dino seemed to have dropped out of show business altogether—aside from hosting an occasional Celebrity Roast. It was as if some Big Brother had retroactively erased him, not just from the airwaves, but from the memories and dreams of the American psyche. We know all there is to know about Elvis and Liberace, not to mention such living fossils as Sinatra and Bob Hope and Don Rickles and Wayne Newton—but Dean Martin? Not a trace. Fifties nostalgia skips right over him, and Andy Warhol never silkscreened his portrait. Scarcely anyone under the age of thirty even knows who he was. It's as if he had disappeared as suddenly and as totally as the dinosaurs; or worse, as if he hadn't ever existed in the first place. We recycle nearly everything else, but there aren't any Dino impersonators around. Dean Martin's story is not the traditional one of a star's rise and fall, not the familiar case of inferior adaptive fitness and lost evolutionary battles. Think rather of him as a singularity, a limit point, a supernova collapsed into a black hole: a fractal discontinuity in the warp and woof of American culture. Think of his disappearance into a haze of alcohol and Alzheimer's as a silent and almost invisible catastrophe: like the disaster of which Blanchot writes, that "takes care of everything," that arrives without ever arriving, and whose violence consists precisely in effacing those very traces that any actual cataclysm would have left behind.

So what happened? Merely to ask such a question, say Deleuze and Guattari, "plays upon a fundamental forgetting ... it places us in relation with something unknowable and imperceptible." *Dino: Living High in the Dirty Business of Dreams*, Nick Tosches' brilliant biography, doesn't restore Dean Martin to collective memory, or place him anew in American cultural life: rather it affirms the inaccessibility of his character, and recapitulates the irreversible erosion of his image. For nothing *can* bring Dino back: his relaxed, sleazy charm is out of sync with the moment, and insensible to nostalgia. The man who cynically crooned "Memories are Made of This," Tosches writes, "hated memory itself." Dino instinctively sought out that primordial oblivion that exceeds and ruins all remembering. "Underneath the feeling in his voice, underneath the weaving of those colors, there was always *lontananza*," the immemorial distance of a past that never has been present, and never can be made present. Elvis may well be the phallus; Dino just "pissed ice water," a less exalted symbolic use of the masculine organ. No matter what he was doing, Tosches says, Dino "never had much interest in this world"; he was "a *menefreghista*—one who simply did not give a fuck." Even in his glory days, the Fifties and early Sixties, Dino seems barely there, a gorgeous, unworldly apparition: the Zen master of the Rat Pack, as Lee Graham calls him. "No one knew him," Tosches writes. "The smart ones took that for granted. To [golfing buddy] Nicky Hilton, Dean was like a beautiful poem that he loved but could never understand."

What Andy Warhol was to the hip New York art and fashion world, Dean Martin was to rootless, suburban Middle America. Martin and Lewis started out playing to sophisticated nightclub audiences in New York and Chicago, but Dino the solo performer flourished in the pleasure palaces of Southern California and Las Vegas. There he unerringly sought out, and slyly, lazily pandered to, whatever was the most "anti-serious, anti-art . . . Dean would become the personification of tastelessness itself, projecting the image of one in whose scale of aesthetics a single good tit joke would outweigh all of Sophocles and Shakespeare" (Tosches). The story is indeed much like Warhol's: Martin, too, is a self-made man, born of immigrant parents, who anglicizes his name, and who achieves fame and fortune through an art that embraces and celebrates American culture at its most commercial and derivative.

And Dino, just like Andy, refuses either to redeem this culture or to critique it. Martin and Warhol both rather *embody* the vulgarity and anonymity of mass culture—in the precise sense that a mirror indifferently embodies whatever has been placed before it. They take all the images offered them and reiterate them to infinity, uncritically, but at a curious second remove. Dean Martin the singer had nothing to express. He was perfectly willing and ready to record any song whatsoever, depending on what the market would bear. Just like Warhol, he let others choose his material for him. He never spent time rehearsing, and never troubled himself to listen to the finished product. Usually, in his stage act, he couldn't even be bothered to finish singing a song that he had started. But no matter what the material, no matter how ludicrous, corny, fake, or inconsequential, his smooth, easygoing voice always "wove it into a lie of gold" (Tosches). The effortless detachment of Dino's singing and acting could well be regarded as a sleazy American version of the spiritual discipline depicted in Eugen Herrigel's *Zen in the Art of Archery*. According to Zen, an art is performed to perfection only when it is unclouded by restless desire, freed of anxiety and of forethought. But this can only be achieved, Herrigel says, "by withdrawing from all attachments whatsoever, by becoming utterly egoless ... by a readiness to yield without resistance." The pupil of Zen "must learn to disregard himself as resolutely as he disregards his opponent," until "the last trace of self-regard vanishes in sheer purposelessness." Well, the only difference between West and East is that Dino didn't need long hours of practice to attain such a state. He had no worldly entanglements to overcome. It just happened naturally. Sinatra, it seems, was an egomaniac and a control freak. But Dino "was not like Frank. He got no thrill from this shit, being onstage, hearing himself on the radio, seeing himself ten feet tall on a screen" (Tosches). Since he really didn't give a fuck, everything just came out right, all by itself.

Dino's songs, therefore, aren't about desire: at least not about the desire that in our culture is commonly figured as 'lack.' They are too relaxed, too casual, too blithely aware of their own insignificance. They have none of the urgency and tension that are the marks of sexual desperation. And they enact none of the melodramatics that typify ungratified yearning. The careless lilt with which Dino suggests "let's fly way up to the clouds" ("Volare") is a rebuke to Romantic myths of the ironic infinitude of desire. And similarly, the deadpan blandness with which Dean in the role of Matt Helm tosses off dumb one-liners in the face of imminent death nullifies all the old claims for tragic dignity, or for high seriousness in art. Forget the castration complex, forget the Hegelian struggle for recognition between master and slave. There is no hint of transcendence, or even of longing for it, anywhere in Dino's act. His songs are suspended rather in the idle hedonism of a blank, dimensionless present: a blurry, contextless realm devoid of antecedent or consequence. They express a sensibility that's perpetually jaded, perhaps, but without any trace of bitterness or disappointment. That's what makes these songs so sensuous and caressing, but also so oddly impersonal and indifferent. Booze and Percodan may have helped, but from the very beginning such was Dino's way. All Dean wanted out of life, Tosches writes, was "a bottle of Scotch, a blowjob, and a million bucks." Nothing else was worth striving for. In Dino's own terms, "that's amore": all ye know on earth, and all ye need to know.

This sublime disinterest is Dean Martin's glory—just as it is Warhol's—and the source of his powers of seduction. It accounts for our sense that, although Dino (just like Elvis) is a pure product *of* American culture, he's somehow (in contrast to Elvis) not altogether *in* it. We desire Elvis because his taut young all-American body seems to contain the living force of all desire. But if we desire Dino—or if our parents once did—it's precisely because he doesn't desire us in return, because he seems to be beyond desire and beyond responsiveness, because clearly he doesn't need us to validate his existence. He has none of Elvis's ambition, none of Elvis's craving for admiration and approval. Dino is the quintessential early-Sixties swinger, carelessly consuming booze and broads, because the spectacles of excess through which he stumbles leave him utterly detached and unaffected—even bored.

Say that his leering 'drunk act' is a glitzy, postmodern, Las Vegas update of Baudelairean dandyism. Or better, say that Dino is the original slacker—so perfectly so, indeed, that today's slacker generation has totally forgotten him. Elvis is retrospectively cool because he was once so hot; his restless soul is always being called back. But Dino's cool is at so low a temperature as to be immune to revivification. Tosches describes it as "a preternatural cool, as divorced from the passing modes of the day as he himself was from the world that in turn embraced and discarded them . . . Dean was an effulgence of the warp between the square and the fashionably cool; and as such, somehow always would elude the fate of the cool, which invariably was to become the square." Dino belongs, then, neither to dialectical History with its ever-evolving fashions, nor to the Eternity that idealist aestheticians imagine to transcend mere fashion. Rather, he moves in another dimension entirely, that of the Nietzschean *untimely*: a "now" too evanescent to be contained by any form of presence, an "unhistorical" stylization that affirms itself at once within and against the ideologies and fashions of the current moment. "This deliberate, difficult attitude consists in recapturing something eternal that is not beyond the present instant, nor behind it, but within it" (Foucault). Dino wondrously combines a suave, refined aesthetic detachment with a calculated wallowing in whatever is most crass. Such an oxymoronic hybridization of sensibilities is his way of expressing the "apotheosis of that which is perishable" (Bataille), or the play of "becoming, the innocence of becoming, forgetting as opposed to memory" (which is how Deleuze and Guattari define the "untimely").

This untimeliness is the key to the mystery of Dean Martin's sudden disappearance. If Elvis, with all his clones, is the triumphant product of processes of natural selection, then Dino is the anomalous, ephemeral, and sterile expression of an illicit counter-movement: of what Brian Massumi calls the forces of "unnatural selection." Memes, like genes, are potentially immortal replicators. But immortality ain't all it's cracked up to be, as Elvis has undoubtedly discovered by now. Timeliness and fame are their own punishments. Your very ubiquity guarantees that you will never again enjoy the thrill of new discoveries and fresh conquests. The hordes of screaming fans no longer bolster your ego; they are just another irritation from which you find it impossible to escape. You can beef up your security, and lock shut the gates to Graceland, but that just makes you feel like a very expensive prisoner. In any case, you've grown bloated and ugly, and every surface you look at turns into a mirror. There's nothing left to do, except sing the same songs to the same crowds in the same casinos, night after night, suspended in an eternal present. Heaven is a place where nothing ever happens. But what's the alternative? Surely nobody believes in the old Romantic myths of damnation any longer. Maybe Elvis OD'd because he thought it would offer him a way out, or at least refurbish his image. But there's nothing more banal than a drug suicide—even that of Sid Vicious has lost whatever transgressive allure it may once have had. If damnation and salvation are binary opposites, this only means that they are virtually indistinguishable. According to Nicole Hollander (*Sylvia*), damnation is indeed a fate worse than death, since Hell is a place "where a medley of Andrew Lloyd Webber tunes is repeated for all eternity." But the distance separating **that** ultimate horror from a steady diet of Late Elvis is, alas, far less than one would hope or imagine.

Evolution is a dead end, even and especially for the survivors. The greater your domination, the more exquisitely fine-tuned your adaptation, the more surely you will stagnate. Lamarckian theories (which assert the inheritance of acquired characteristics, and thus the possibility of continual self-improvement) are wrong: for even the most advantageous mutations only come about *in spite of* a species' genetic and cultural 'striving,' rather than because of it. In nature as in Hollywood, the big money is always being invested in sequels and remakes. Remember the words of the sage in the Borges story: "mirrors and copulation are abominable, because they increase the number of men." The problem is not that we live in a world of simulacra, as Baudrillard so naively thinks. No: the problem is that nothing is ever simulacral and inauthentic enough.

The copies, the impersonators, remain all too loyal to their models. What would it take to imagine a simulacrum that, as Deleuze wishes, "denies at once both the original and the copy, the model and the reproduction"? Not a faithful rendition of Elvis, nor a critical parody of Elvis, but a performance that is more "Elvis" than Elvis himself ever was: only this can release the singer from the torment of his own endlessly repeated identity. But what could it mean to will—to select, in a Darwinian sense—your own divergence, your own alteration, even your own extinction? "Man is something that must be overcome," Zarathustra cries; "what have you done to overcome him?" And according to Severo Sarduy, the "hidden goal" of camouflage, in fashion as in combat, in humans as much as in insects, is less adaptation and survival than "a kind of disappearance, invisibility, *effacement* and erasure." Zarathustra thus praises those who "want to perish of the present," whose very "life is a going-under." But doesn't Dean Martin embody such a counter-teleology, both in his life and in his art? Isn't his sterile hedonism a rebuke to the horrors of infinity and eternity and all-too-faithful reflections? Martini in hand, let us then embark on Dino's way, and embrace his strategies of disappearance. After all, as Tosches suggests, that's what we Americans do the best: "Dean was the American spirit at its truest: fuck Vietnam, fuck politics, fuck morality, fuck culture, and fuck the counter-culture, fuck it all. We were here for but a breath; twice around the fountain and into the grave: fuck it."

What more is there to say? Elvis may well be the Savior; but Dino offers us no redemption, not even one "in quotation marks." In his retirement, he was more untimely than ever, exiled as he was from the New Hollywood of cellular phones and twelve-step programs. Why, in 1988, the last time they reviewed him in *Variety*, they even complained about his lack of "social consciousness over the unfunny aspects of intoxication"! Can you believe it? Don't look to Dino for lessons in temperance, or foresight, or heroism, or any of the other virtues. You won't find him singing on a UFO, or giving advice in the toilet. But isn't that precisely his greatness? As his ex-wife Jeanne sums it up for Tosches: "Dean can do nothing better than anyone in the world. He can literally do nothing . . . He was always content in a void." Dino's very untimeliness makes him more postmodern than any of us. That great decentering, that crumbling of the foundations, so often approached with anguish and loathing—well, Dino *lived* it for years, no problem, without a trace of anxiety. Tosches gives us a final picture of Dean Martin in old age, watching Westerns on TV, and sipping glass after glass of wine: "every swallow brought breath that bore neither memory nor meaning nor even deliverance from them—he no longer needed that deliverance—but rather the strange sweetness of something that may or may not have ever been." Memory has become indistinguishable from fiction; and redemption, or the lack thereof, just isn't an issue any more. Yes, the world has receded into its own flickering image, and nothing is true or false any longer, and it's very late, and the TV has been on for hours. But what's the matter with that? Images proliferate endlessly in the void, regardless of whether anyone is there looking at them or not. You don't watch programs *on* TV; you simply watch TV. Turn down the volume and go to bed, there'll be something else in the morning.

Index

Serpent's Tail

1986 to 1996

TEN YEARS WITH ATTITUDE!

"If you've got hold of a book that doesn't fit the categories
and doesn't miss them either,
the chances are that you've got a serpent by the tail."

ADAM MARS-JONES

"The Serpent's Tail boldly goes
where no reptile has gone before ... More power to it!"

MARGARET ATWOOD

If you would like to receive a catalogue of our current publications please write to:

FREEPOST, Serpent's Tail,
4 Blackstock Mews, LONDON N4 2BR

(No stamp necessary if your letter is posted in the United Kingdom.)